An Ordinary Farm Girl Meets an Extra-ordinary God.

Author

Pearl Tadema M.Ed.

PRESS

TABLE OF CONTENTS

Dedication

To my children, grandchildren, and great-grandchildren.

How fun it would be to sit under a big maple tree and share all God's doings in my life with each one of you individually. But since all forty-three of you, my unique grandchildren, are adding spouses regularly, plus an ever increasing number of precious great-grandchildren I thought it best to write my thoughts so you could read them at your leisure.

My Mom and Dad wrote briefly the story of God's faithfulness in their lives. Getting to know some of their adventures in faith has encouraged me to trust God more. Now it's my turn to encourage you to experience God's reality for yourself. Hopefully some of you will be inspired as I was, to record your spiritual episodes too. Then our family can have a record of God "showing love to a thousand generations of those who love me and keep my commandments." (Exodus 20:6, NIV)

The incidents I'm picking from my life show how God Himself directed my life's little sailboat. There were squalls and thunderstorms testing my ability to sail. I found myself more and more often consulting His Sailing Manual (the Bible). When I didn't consult Him disaster splashed against my face. Also, I discovered that God actually does smooth out rough waters for those who love Him.

I'm writing this in the hopes of boosting your faith, and I pray that the wind of the Holy Spirit will keep your sails full as God leads you along to His harbor.

Love,

Great-Beppe Pearl Tadema.
Spokane, Washington

Acknowledgments.

My first acknowledgement is to the Holy Spirit who kept bugging me to leave a stone of remembrance for our grandchildren as Joshua was commanded to do in Joshua 4:4-9. His twelve stones served as a sign to remember how God dried up the Jordan to let three million of His people cross over. My book is a remembrance of how faithful God was to us as a family, and will be to our posterity.

The little writer's groups we attended were a huge encouragement for me to continue. Rits, my husband, kept saying, "You can do it", and helped improve wording, plus the pats on the back, which were worth more than words.

Chaplain Stroud, DeeDee Price, Patti Padgett, Hessel and Heather Baker, the Leaps, and many more gave me impetus to get it in print.

Thank you all, and here it is!

CHAPTER ONE:

BEGINNINGS START LIVES UNIQUELY.

Does how and to whom we are born matter?

The Zylstra Family In Ogilvie, Minnesota

Mom took this picture.

An older Paul had drowned. An older Simon had died of pneumonia. Andrew and Bertha not yet born.

This is the nest out of which she flew into marriage with Daddy.

After I was married Mom and I went for a ride in Monroe. She pointed to an old two story white house saying, "That's where you were born."

I said, "How can that be? I thought you told me I was born in the Monroe Hospital."

She laughed and replied, "That was the Monroe Hospital June 24, 1929. I had to stay there for two weeks because I had toxemia when you were born. I didn't get to hold you for twelve days. Dad came to see me every day after working in the Sultan Saw Mill. He said afterward that I was very sick and he prayed much that I would recover.

"Good thing! I can't imagine life without you Mom. How old were you when you had me?"

"I was nineteen when we got married, and you were born when I was twenty. Right after marriage we honey mooned from Minnesota to Sultan, Washington. We were poor but very happy.

"How is it Mom that you got to know Daddy, and why did you fall in love with him? Of course we love him, he's the best Daddy in the whole wide world."

"Daddy was milking cows in Wisconsin but got homesick for his brother John and for the Christian Reformed Church so he moved back to Ogilvie area. He had come to America as a sixteen year old with his Uncle Louie and his fourteen year old brother Irvin, and his 18 year old brother Walter. His brother John was in the Netherlands army at the time. Uncle Louie settled on a little farm in the Ogilvie-Pease area and the boys worked for him to pay off their boat fare. When Dad was in Wisconsin John immigrated also.

"I met Dad at the Young People's Society at the Church. I was thrilled when he took me home one night. I liked him right away. We dated four years, and all along he was my knight in shining armour. He was everything a woman could want. I guess I fell in love with him right off the bat, and the love just grew and got stronger."

"I know that Pa died and you and Daddy took in Ma and all your siblings, but just how did that happen? I was only two and just figured that this was normal."

"My youngest sister, Bertha, was born in Minnesota when you were six months old. Shortly after that Pa (my dad) and Ma

Mom and Daddy coming to Washingtn on their Honeymoon.

(my mom) moved from Minnesota to Washington with their nine children and six cows. Pa rode in the cattle car of the train with the cows, and Ma kept the nine children happy with sandwiches she had taken along.

"They stayed with the three of us in our three bedroom rented farmhouse along with Uncle Louie and wife Moike, who also moved from Minnesota and joined us while he was looking for work."

"What a lot of work for you Mom! How did you ever manage all that?"

"For one thing Uncle Louie took down the walls of the woodshed and made a long table for our large family of seventeen. We fit like sardines in a can! All the boys slept in the attic with the bats. They threw pillows at the bats until they were tired enough to sleep. My sister Rena, two years younger than me, soon got a job doing housework and that made us sixteen. But after several months both Louie and Pa found little farms to rent.

Pa complained plenty of headaches for several months. At the hospital they found he had a malignant brain tumor, and he soon died. You were eighteen months and Bertha a year."

Pearl two years

Aunt Bertha, one and a half years

"Daddy and I felt like God wanted us to assume responsibility for Ma and her nine children. We moved into Ma's house since it had one more bedroom, and Daddy assumed Pa's debt and his six cows, which he added to the two cows he had recently acquired. Sadie was born in this same year."

"Wow Mom! You got a huge family in short order. And you were only married three years! I guess. I just figured this was normal. Now I understand why Andrew didn't know you were his sister until he was nine years old."

"Since I was oldest I was somewhat prepared for added responsibility because Ma could never organize housework very well, so

Daddy with first car and first cow.

at an early age, I did a lot of the housework while she was having babies. I figured that was just the way life was."

"Mom, I used to get irritated with how you tried to make us be as organized as you."

"Yah, I know it wasn't always fun. But Ma would have been a better mother if she had been more systematic. I guess God was preparing me for helping them out when Pa died."

"I realize now Mom, that those skills enabled you to garden and sew so well that you got all of us through the Depression without realizing we were poor. So often when we came home from school you would be sitting at the sewing machine. Without turning your head you would say Pearl do this, or Sadie do that. And what you were doing was making my dolly a little coat with real buttons and loop buttonholes. I don't know how you managed that when you made me a lovely wool jacket that itched like crazy, you made us three girls dresses from printed sacks, and made the boys' wool pants and jackets out of old suits given to you. And you did all that without a pattern."

"I couldn't afford a pattern, so I looked at how the adult suits were made and followed suit. Making do was always a creative challenge for me. It made me feel good when I succeeded."

"I appreciate you so much more now than when I was a kid. Oh Mom, I took so much for granted."

Death is cheated.

When I was two, Ma (grandma…we all called her Ma) and my Mom were washing with the gas Maytag on the porch. Water was heated on a wood stove and Mom had set a pail of boiling water down for a moment. Somehow I backed into it and was severely burned from waist to knees. My life hung in the balance while my parents prayed for their God to have mercy on little Pearl. God was so merciful that after fifteen days I could return home from the hospital.

All I remember of the incident was that a visitor, when I was four, asked to see my scars. Mom lifted my dress, and I was so mortified I hid behind her and cried. After that I was ashamed for anyone to see me naked.

Can God see me?

Mom read Bible stories in the evening to us kids including Bertha. She said, "God sees everything."

I hid behind the couch and said, "Can He see me here?"

She said, "Yes, He can see you".

I hid in the closet and shouted, "Can he see me here, through the door?"

She said, "Yes, He sees everything."

Later, playing hide-and-go-seek, I hid in the hay and thought, *"God can even see me here under the hay where no one else can find me."* I was comforted. I thought about it again as a first grader when the bus left without me, and I sat on the sidewalk and cried. A teacher came by and asked me if I knew the way home. I said, "Yes."

She said, "Will you quit crying if I take you home in my car?"

I jumped up, wiped the tears on my dress, and felt oh so proud riding in her car, telling her where to go, and feeling very, very special. *Yes, God is seeing me all the time.*

When I was older and babysitting the younger siblings at night, I was terrified hearing the old house creak and I thought, *"Maybe the house is on fire."* Over and over I'd calm my pounding heart with, *"God is seeing us. He cares."* To be seen is to feel significant.

In 1933 Daddy found a farm with two houses, and we moved to Carnation. Now Ma and her children had a house of their own. We all went to Ma's place at teatime, three o'clock every day. She baked bread buns, and smeared them with butter and blackberry jam. One for each of us, and if we were late our bun would wait for us on the table. Ahh! How tantalizing was the aroma of fresh baked bread. We loved teatime.

Conversation centered mostly on cows, calves, grain, hay, manure, price of milk, milk inspectors, and relatives. If someone did well in school that was mentioned. Never was my naughtiness mentioned at 'tea time'. Teatime was such fun.

When the blackberries ripened we all picked because we could sell them at the local store. Rena came home to pick blackberries in order to buy a new dress. She was the fastest picker, and put her first crate in the shade, away from the fence. I was copying how Clarence picked because he was next fastest. Then I heard Rena scream, "You dirty thief, you dirty thief," and I saw her run across the pasture as fast as she could, arms waving. She was just too late. A cow had stretched her neck through the wire and licked up all her berries.

Sundays the Packard car was piled full of passengers for Church in Duvall, ten miles away. We couldn't all get in, so this one Sunday I had to stay home with Simon and Andrew. They decided to go fishing, a forbidden activity when the folks were not home. After finding worms we walked out on a big log lying in a 'lake' that was nearby. This 'lake' was formed by floodwaters from the nearby river.

Uncles swim where I fell off the log.

Simon caught a fish and yelled, "Get off the log. Hurry up! Get off."

I turned, lost my balance, and fell in. I do remember feeling the bottom and thinking, 'This must be the way up'. I walked upwards on the squishy bottom. The moment my hair floated to the top Simon grabbed it and yanked me out.

In despair he looked at me and said, "Your dress is wet. Your folks will know we disobeyed." He grabbed my hand and said, "We'll run until it's dry." We ran and ran up and down the driveway and across the pasture until my side ached.

I said, "I have to stop, my side aches."

Panic in his voice he said, "We can't stop. Your dress isn't dry. They'll soon be home. We'll get in trouble." He jerked me forward and we ran more. He was ten and I five. I couldn't keep up.

Finally, my side hurt so much I jerked my hand out of his and grabbed my side. I said, "I'll take the spankings. Please, I can't run any more."

What was he thinking? Did he think my dress made out of the cheap cotton sacks with-flowers printed on would look like it was ironed when dry? Of course, Mom saw my wrinkled dress right away even though it was dry by then and knew I had fallen in the water. She seemed to be possessed of a sixth sense that invariably discovered disobedience. Seemed like I never got by with anything! This day neither Simon nor I got in trouble: maybe because visitors came home with the folks from church.

In 1935 as soon as the rent contract on that farm was up, we moved to Duvall on a hundred and forty eight acre farm. I was finishing up first grade. My new teacher didn't seem to like me. I ached for the Tolt teacher who let me read to her at recess with one arm around me. I felt displaced and decided to not like this school. Bad decision.

Daddy soon accumulated eighty-six cows and my Uncles worked for him. We all had jobs to do. Because I loved the outdoors and the barn, I fed the barn-cats, and chickens, pushed hay in front of the cows, and taught newborn calves how to drink from a bucket. Later, Daddy trusted me to strip cows, milk a couple who did not tolerate the milking-machine, dump milk into the cooler, and spin ten gallon milk cans outside for the milk truck to pick up. When my chores were done, I curled up in the hay with a book and got lost in a world of make-believe. I knew if I went to the house Mom would have plenty of work for me.

The big white horse does it all.

One spring when I was nine Daddy was plowing the second field with a big white horse, Slim, and the mule, Coin. Mom asked me to bring him a thermos of coffee and a couple cookies out in the field. As I approached I noticed that Slim was lathered with sweat, but Coin walking in the furrow was not only not sweating, but was walking precisely half a step behind Slim. I said, "Daddy, do you see that Slim does all the work, and Coin is not really pulling? You should whack Coin on the rump and make him do his share."

Daddy smiled and said, "I know Pearl. Slim loves to work. Look at him paw the ground. He can hardly wait until I'm done drinking my coffee. I need Coin to hold up his end of the yoke so we can plow a straight line. Look, half the pasture is already plowed. I have a good team."

Years later when I was sweating things, I thought back on this incident as a perfect illustration of Jesus' words, "Come to Me all you who labor and are heavy laden, and I will give you rest. For My yoke is easy, and My burden is light." (Matthew 11:28, 30.)

Jesus is the big white horse who loves to work. Like Coin our only job is to hold up our end of the yoke and walk a half step behind Jesus so we don't sweat, and so we travel together a straight line to heaven. What a great plan God has."

Daddy plowing with Slim and mule Coin

In school, I met a girl who only had one brother. I felt so sorry for her. She had no one to play Hide-and-seek with, Kick-the-can, or Baseball. What would I do without all my Uncles who let me play with them? Even worse she had no one to sleep with on a load of hay. I had sister Sadie, Bertha, and neighbor Lois. We'd giggle, watch the stars 'fall', and talk about feeling something bob on our chests when riding on a wagon.

In the summer, I participated in jobs like weeding the garden, driving round and round the field tedding hay, or driving the tractor in compound low while the uncles pitched hay on the wagons. Saturdays Sadie and I washed the car, polished our shoes, changed the sheets on our beds, and did whatever else my mom dreamt up.

Sadie, Bertha and I managed to find time to fish for suckers in the Snoqualmie River which ran in front of the house, or play house under the vine maples on the river bank. Bertha and Sadie were always the Moms who took their crying, sick babies to me the doctor who gave medicine or put splints on their broken bones.

On a nice sunny summer day, about 1939 Sadie, Bertha and I drove an old truck to the end of our farm, put some gunny sacks under our arms and walked a half mile to little Round Lake in our neighbor's woods. We'd find cascara trees, climb them and with a jack knife strip off the bark. With our gunny sacks full we'd drag them back to the truck. One day the truck ran out of water and heated up. We got out and looked in all the ditches. No water. I said, "I got an idea. Let's all pee in this old coffee can, and put it in the radiator. That should get us home." And it did.

We then emptied our gunnysacks onto the roof of the woodshed to dry in the sun. We chipped them in about one-inch chips and brought them to the store manager who bought our stash for ten cents a pound. We felt down right rich. But the sun doesn't always shine in western Washington, and when it rained and our cascara bark got too wet or moldy our great expectations were crushed.

Sometimes the Uncles would be working hard bringing in hay, and Daddy would say, "Enough hard work."

The Uncles invariably responded, "But we're almost done, we can finish before dark:"

Daddy answered, "Accidents happen when everybody gets tired. We're all going swimming at Cottage Lake!" Other days we'd go on a picnic up Stevens Pass. All of these activities gave me the feeling of being a necessary part of the whole family. I belonged, and felt secure in that belonging.

Family Picnic at Steven's Pass, 1939

Sin?

On a sunny day, Bertha, Sadie, Lois (our neighbor girlfriend) and I were smoking dock seed rolled in Lois' Dad's cigarette papers behind the barn. We were coughing and laughing wondering what men saw in smoking. Lois' oldest brother came by and said, "If you sneak some of Dad's real tobacco, you might enjoy it."

We had "borrowed" a few cigarette papers, but we would never think of sneaking her Dad's tobacco! That would be stealing plain and simple.

Then to our horror, he pulled out his penis, a very large one to the eyes of eight to ten year old girls and ejaculated in front of us. Shocked and grossed out we told him, "Go away, weirdo." He left laughing. We poked at the semen with a stick making remarks like, "'Oh Yuk. How weird. Why would he do a thing like that?"

Later when Daddy read in the Bible about Onan spilling his seed on the ground, I knew it was indeed strange behavior. And yes, it must be sin. I had never thought much about sin. For the first time I felt real repulsion against sin.

I did not trust him from then on and I thought: *Do other men do that? Not my uncles, they wouldn't do anything that stupid.*

I was about twelve doing my chores in the barn, when a hired man beat on a cow with a 2x4. I yelled at him to stop. He yelled back, "She kicked me, and I'll beat the _____out of her." He hit her again and again until blood dropped off her rear. She groaned, eyes wild with helplessness. He hit her over, and over and she bellered an anguished loud cry jerking her neck against the unrelenting stanchion trying to escape. Then he grabbed her tail and twisted it until it broke.

I was livid and shouted, "You have no right to beat a helpless animal like that."

Through tight lips he looked at me, a glaze over his eyes, and said, "Maybe you need a lesson or two." And he took after me with the 2x4 raised! Being skinnier and not carrying a 2x4 I slipped through stanchions and out a narrow opening in the back door. I ran behind the granary, across the road, down the riverbank, and under the pump house. When I saw he had not followed, I wept with relief. What happened to this pleasant, happy man who played baseball with us?

Squeezed under the pump house on my belly, the smell of dirty sand, and grease making an indelible impression, I came to three conclusions, which would haunt me later. 1. Never confront a person who is angry about the truth. 2. The best tact when someone is angry is to run away. 3. Run away before their eyes are glazed over otherwise they might kill you.

I couldn't stay squished under their forever. I needed to finish my chores. I crawled out, peeked in the barn and saw Daddy there.

With a sigh of relief I went back to work. The hired man acted as if nothing had happened. He was his usual cheerful self and I was flabbergasted. It baffled me how a person could be so bedeviling, my feelings scraped raw over the imminent blow he intended. I never told anybody, for I had enough trouble for one day. Sunken somewhere out of reach of my heart was a yawning cavern where I stuffed the feelings of rejection and the three misconstrued conclusions. I was sure if I hadn't outrun him, I no doubt would have been horribly hurt or dead.

Death enters my life.

Mom gave birth to a baby sister. The baby died the same day she was born. At the graveside service, Daddy asked that they open the little coffin so we could say 'goodbye'. She was perfect. Her face like a dolly's face, and a pretty ruffled dress made her look like she only needed to be awakened. Many nights I dreamt that I went to the graveyard and with bare hands dug up her tiny coffin, and woke her up!

A mile and a half down the road lived a farm family with their two-year-old toddler, Johnny. On an afternoon he disappeared. They looked all through the barns, outbuildings, and ditches. Finally, they looked in the river across the road, the most feared place, and one that they assumed he could not access. They didn't find him, but others got boats and searched along the banks. The next day someone found him snagged by a branch some distance down stream, his face peaceful in death.

This was the second time I was confronted by human death. From this time on, I had nightmares in which I was caught by the current, swept along, and drowning. I woke up when my breath was gone, and I knew I was on the verge of death. Some fifty years later I had an experience of near drowning that ended these nightmares.

Fifth grade shenanigans are forgiven.

My fifth grade teacher told the class she was giving us an extra long recess time. We were to come in when she rang the bell ten times. We were all playing baseball when the bell rang nineteen

26

times! Two others and I refused to go in because the bell did not ring ten times. I felt very justified. My two friends finally went in. But I held my ground until school was out. *She should do what she said she was going to do.*

I totally forgot about God seeing me. Finally, I thought I should get my lunch bucket and be ready to board the bus. But the minute I entered the schoolroom, the teacher commanded me, "Go to your seat, and stay there until I say you can get up."

The bus left without me. She raised her voice; "I'm going to punish you for disobedience."

I reminded her respectfully, "I was not disobedient to the ten rings you promised." She got red in the face and hit me with a yardstick. Then she missed and hit the desk breaking her yardstick. I tried not to laugh. Now with fury she ordered me into the cloakroom where with a new yardstick she began beating me on the legs. She couldn't hurt me. I stood still and let her do her thing. This only increased her rage. Finally out of breath, she sat at her desk and wrote a letter to my parents.

I thought: *"I knew this school was stupid."*

She said, "You cannot come back to school until I get a note from your parents. Now walk home and take this letter to your parents."

Walking the three miles home I thought: *its best I read what she has written.* I dropped the letter in a mud puddle so I could unseal it. What she wrote about my rebellious attitude would not be good for my parents to read. So I dropped it in a squishy cow pie. The ink was getting nice and blurry, but this would be rather hard to explain.

When I got home, I handed Mom the manuscript, and she hung it over the wood stove to dry. She said, "We'll talk to Daddy when he comes in from the barn." The uncles who attended the same small school had already told on me. I thought, *having Uncles is sometimes a pain.*

When she left the kitchen, I dropped the letter in the hot stove. *There is no doubt I am completely justified in what I did, so why am I treated like I'm bad?*

When Daddy came in, he squeezed my arm just below the shoulder with powerful fingers that had milked thirty cows by hand twice a day. My arm got numb. Daddy had my full attention. He said, "You knew when everybody went in you should too. You've made your teacher's job difficult, and that is not Christian."

Tears spurted out of my eyes. My self-justification melted like ice in hot tea. All I wanted was to get my arm back, and stop Daddy's discipline. I said, "Yes, Daddy." And he let me go.

The next morning I said, "I can't go back to school without a note."

Daddy said, "What shall I write in this note?"

I said, "That I'm sorry, and will try to be a Christian girl."

Daddy did not seal the envelope.

God gets my attention through Mrs. Ramsey, Daddy and Simon.

The next year, we had a new teacher. Mrs. Ramsey taught spelling while I read a Big Little Book behind my spelling lessons. Flash Gordon and his space exploits far exceeded spelling in excitement. She said, "Pearl will you take the next word?" I didn't have a clue. She came to my desk and took the Big Little Book, which I had borrowed, and pointed to the word she wanted me to read.

At recess she called me to her desk and said, "Pearl, I have a better book for you to read. This Big Little Book adds nothing to your education. Here's Pilgrim's Progress and when you finish it, I will give you back your Big Little Book."

With heavy heart I took the book, but all my thoughts were on the boy I borrowed the Big Little Book from and how he was looking at me. I read Pilgrim's Progress as fast as I could by hiding in the hay to escape Mom's chores. I was three-fourths done before I could admit that it had some good parts.

Mrs. Ramsey questioned me on it, gave me back my borrowed book, and then said, "Come Pearl, I want to show you some books that are truly more exciting than Flash Gordon." She took me to the library and showed me a book with pictures of Crater Lake and said, "It has no bottom. Read all about it." Then she asked me, "Have you ever seen stars fall?"

I said, "Yes, sleeping in the hay I've seen many."

She pointed to a shelf with books on the stars and galaxies asking me, "What really happens when they fall?"

Thanks to Mrs. Ramsey I soon wanted to read all the books in the library. And in spite of not wanting to like school, I liked it in my heart. I never should have decided to not like this school.

One very dark night Daddy and I were feeling our way along the road walking from barn to house. He said, "I think the three days of darkness in the land of Egypt couldn't be much darker than this. Imagine no house with electricity, and not knowing how many days it would stay dark!"

I thought: *Daddy knows every single Bible story is true!*

Yes, every day Daddy read a chapter from the Bible at breakfast, dinner and supper. When we ended Revelation, he started all over. I asked him one day, "Why not skip all those names, endless descriptions of sacrifices and numbers of people?"

He answered, "God inspired people to write it for a reason. God said it would be profitable for us to read it." In spite of some daydreaming, over the years much of it sank in, especially respect for God's Words.

Often Simon, four years older than I, ran the milking machines while I was stripping some of the cows. (Stripping was milking by hand the last of the milk out of a cow after the milking machine had done the first part. This was done when we first got milking machines and the cows were not used to it. Nobody does it today.) We talked about what might be beyond the Milky Way. Was heaven out there somewhere, and could Jesus actually drop out of the clouds today?

Simon went out to chase up some more cows from the holding pen. Someone had put the bull in there, and I saw him turn to butt Simon. He was pinning Simon with Simon's back against the fence! I gasped, watching the bull smack his head against Simon's stomach! But suddenly Simon was sitting on top of the fence out of reach of the bull.

With an ashen face, his brown eyes wide open, he entered the barn and I asked him, "How in the world did you get on top of the fence so quickly? I thought the bull already had you pinned."

He said, "I didn't. Just all of a sudden I was there, out of reach."

I said, "An angel!" We both smiled. He nodded. We never told anybody because we did not want to be disbelieved. It was obvious to me that angels are real.

The turning point of my life is eternal.

We had a new pastor in Duvall, 1943, who had been a missionary in China. Rev. Dykstra wanted everybody to know for sure they were saved. He, therefore, insisted that the young people memorize the entire Heidelberg Catechism. It consisted of fifty-two sections called Lord's Days, one for each week. Usually there were three questions in each Lord's Day. Numerous scriptures substantiated the answers. Pastors were required to preach on one each Sunday.

He gave me special permission to start the class though I was not the required fifteen years old. The rest of the class had memorized each question and answer during that year, but were now reviewing them two Lord's Days at a time. I wanted to keep up with the class, so I typed the questions and answers in school and pinned them on the knee of my overalls when stripping cows. The old cows were not used to the machine, so I went after the machine to strip the last of the milk out.

With my head on the cow's belly, and the bucket between my knees, I whispered, ___*What is your only comfort in life and death?*___ Then I'd peek at my cards and mumble into the cow's belly, "That I, with body and soul, both in life and in death, am not my own, but belong to my faithful Savior, Jesus Christ;"…

"*Do I really belong?* I asked myself. I poured some milk in the kitty dish, and moved to the next cow. "Who with His precious blood has fully satisfied for all my sins, and delivered me from all the power of the devil;"

"*I know He died for the sins of the whole world, but I still sin so I'm obviously not delivered from the power of the devil.*"

"And so preserves me that without the will of my heavenly Father not a hair can fall from my head;"…

"*Well, I know He sees everything, so He knows how many hairs Mom pulled out of my head when she was braiding my hair, but that couldn't possibly be important to the God who runs the Universe.*"

" Yea, that all things are subservient to my salvation, wherefore by His Holy Spirit He also assures me of eternal life, and makes me heartily willing and ready henceforth to live unto Him."

"I wonder how the Holy Spirit will let me know. How does He assure? How will I know if I have eternal life?"

Every week new questions and answers piled up, one pile on top of the other like making a stack of hay for the winter. One thing bothered me: *"could all this really be for me, a non-descript little farm girl?"*

The pastor said it was important to "invite Jesus into your life," so every night and often during the day I asked Jesus to come into my life. I didn't have a clue how He was going to do this, or how I would know if He did. Months went by and I didn't let up on the memorizing, but the nagging doubt that all this was for "little me" hung around like the smell of manure.

Finally, we were to memorize 1 John 5:12-13, a proof text for the questions and answers of the week. "He who has the Son has life; he who does not have the Son of God does not have life."

As I squirted milk into the mouth of a beggar kitty, I wondered, *"Do I have this life? I don't want to do without it."*

"These things I have written to you who believe in the name of the Son of God." *I believe everything I've been memorizing. It has to be true, Daddy and Mom believe it is true.*

"That you may know that you have eternal life, and that you may continue to believe in the name of the Son of God."

*I have eternal life! I have eternal life! It says right here that all I've been memorizing is so **that I may know.***

It was like the Holy Spirit tapped me on the shoulder that was against the cow's thigh and whispered; "Now you <u>know</u> you have eternal life." I was so happy I began to sing hymns.

One uncle asked me why I sang in the cracks and changed key. I didn't know he was talking about singing between the white keys of the piano. After a couple of hours another uncle said, "Do you have to sing all the time?"

Would they laugh at me if I told them, "Now I know I have eternal life?" I didn't take a chance on telling them.

I didn't tell anybody because I was afraid they'd say, "of course, I already knew that', and then maybe my joy would go away. But I did want people who didn't go to Church or memorize catechism to know that God was offering eternal life through Jesus. So I thought of offering Bibles to all the homes in Duvall, about sixty then. I asked Bertha to go with me, but she said she was scared, so I went alone.

I walked to Duvall and got six Bibles from Church, and knocked on the first door saying, "I'll give you this Bible if you would like to know how to get eternal life."

He said, "Hell, no. I've got enough trouble with this life!" He shut the door before I could say another word.

At the next door I said to the lady, "If you would like to know how to get to heaven, I'll give you this free Bible."

She said, "Thanks, but I already have two Bibles." Whew! That was better.

At the third door I said the same thing about getting to heaven and he said, "What makes you think God cares about anybody? If He's up there why doesn't He stop these stupid wars? Why did He let my kid get killed?" I didn't know what to say. He said louder, "Take your Bibles away. God doesn't give a dam." I was glad to leave.

At the next house I got bolder and said, "What is your only comfort in life and death? This Bible has the answer. You can have it for free if you want to know". The man said, "Lord knows we could use some comfort." And he took a Bible. That's better!

Encouraged I took the same tact at the fifth house. This man said, "I've read it and got no comfort at all. I suppose you're one of those that don't believe in evolution either. Me, I'll take scientific fact." What could I say? I felt dumb. He continued his tirade proving beyond doubt my stupidity.

Finally, his wife came and said, "He doesn't want a Bible. Just leave."

At the sixth house, nobody answered my knock, and I gave a sigh of immense relief! I walked the three miles home with five Bibles still under my arm. Why didn't everybody want a Bible? I was perplexed and hurt, and glad Bertha was not along. I thought, *I'll have to know how to answer their objections before I do this again.*

Missionary stories impact my life.

Daddy ordered the National Geographic Magazine. I was fascinated by the pigmies and wondered if their smallness made them feel out of place as my being the tallest in school sometimes did. Some of the kids in school took over my uncles' jibes calling me beanpole, long legs, telephone pole, or spider long legs. Their ridicule made me feel like they wanted me to be a misfit. However, I knew in my heart that I was the size God wanted me to be.

Daddy also got a book called White Queen of the Cannibals. Mary Slessor was a tomboy and went alone to the natives in Africa to tell the Good News. And I thought: *I can do that! Wouldn't that be an adventure?*

Then Daddy brought a book home called Johanna Veenstra, Pioneer Missionary to Africa. She was the first woman missionary who went out alone from our Christian Reformed Denomination. I thought: *I can do that.* Inspired by their lives, I became an avid reader of missionary stories.

Sometimes while stripping cows I'd catch up with the 'machine-milkers'. Then I'd sit on my stool, which was strapped to my rear, lean against the wall behind the cows and take down a book hanging there on 'Diseases and Problems of Large Farm Animals.' It was intriguing to find out how to heal 'milk fever' with an intravenous Ca-Mg drip, how to go in up to ones arm pits to turn a calf trying to be birthed the wrong way, how to get barbed wire out of a cow's stomach with a magnet, and how to stick a knife into a cow's abdomen to relieve the bloat.

Leaning against my favorite cow with her big brown eyes, I thought: *I can combine my interest in medical things with being a missionary. David Livingston did. Yes, if I worked very hard, I could do that.*

Shortly after that thought, I heard a sermon challenging us to make a commitment to read one chapter in the Bible a day for one year. *I can do that.* I promised God I'd do it. I forgot to write down the date so I never knew when my year was over. Good thing: I didn't dare break my promise to God and so reading a chapter a day became such a habit I've continued it for sixty-four years now.

One night I was reading my chapter and it was about how the disciples couldn't cure the epileptic boy, so Jesus did. They asked, "Why couldn't we do it?"

Jesus said, "Because you have so little faith. I tell you the truth, if you have faith as small as a mustard seed, you can say to this mountain, 'Move from here to there' and it will move. Nothing will be impossible for you."

I thought: Can this be really true? Of course it's true. Jesus said it. But does anybody do such things? While I was going round and round the field with the tractor tedding hay, I looked at the nearby hill and thought: *I'm a long ways from having faith to tell that hill to drop into Puget Sound! But would I have faith to tell the cedar tree on top of the hill to topple over? No, it isn't my tree. However, we have a cedar tree on our land. But then I'd have to have a very good purpose to see it toppled. I guess I have neither faith nor purpose for such things, but this is an amazing verse!*

My Love for Horses meets a need.

Daddy used mules and horses for farming before the coming of our B-John Deere. I went to the horse stalls daily in the summer. I was drawn there by the smell of horse manure -like sweet garden soil. I wanted to help harness them, but they were frisky and Daddy wouldn't let me. However, I lifted the heavy collar handing it to Daddy. The leather felt smooth as velvet where the horses sweat rubbed the collar against their hide.

After a day's work they stood still waiting to be relieved of their harnesses. Their sweat, like whipping cream, bunched up around the straps. It smelled and felt like the foam on milk, only thicker. I also liked to feel the contrast of soft nose and the sinewy muscles spiraling down their legs. I think I liked them because I admired their strength.

Daddy let me ride a still wet Tommy from the stall to the pasture. I headed toward the back of the first pasture trying to get an exhilarating ride. This broad Belgian trotted reluctantly and roughly in response to my kicking his sides as best I could across his wide back. He'd put in a day's work and resented my demands. In response to a slap on his rear with the reins he lurched into a gallop.

Whee! I clung with hands firmly twisted in his mane. Near the end of the field he stopped on a dime, turned on that same dime and flung me off into the clover pasture. Then he'd trot home looking back with a sneer, or was it a laugh? It happened every time I was privileged to take him to pasture, and every time I was sure that next time I'd stay on. I had the idea that if I could just stay on and be Boss then I'd be stronger than he.

I wanted a riding horse like the neighbor kids who had Shetland ponies. Each time Daddy went for groceries I put 'horse' on the end of the grocery list. Daddy reminded me that a riding horse was simply an expense—what good was this expense?

In the meantime I rode Coin, our mule, with the neighbor kids. Coin was not competitive. I was. He didn't care if all the kids were half a mile ahead of us. I did. Their ponies obediently jumped a shallow ditch or walked through it. Coin saw no need. He'd look back at me seeming to ask, "'Why this?" The only time I excelled with him was picking cherries: he was twice as tall as the other ponies. He also liked just standing.

Coin's back was like riding on the side of a two by four. An hour of bouncing on that and I was convinced I needed a saddle. Realistically, I needed a horse and saddle. I told Daddy, "It is worth the expense."

Between my freshman and sophomore years a truck arrived on our yard. They unloaded a reddish riding horse with a saddle. What a Daddy. Redwing and I rode and rode all over the farm and neighboring farms. In my fantasy I was galloping over the wide-open prairie. In reality I galloped over one cow pasture and stopped to open and close a gate to the next and the next.

I whispered secrets in Redwings ear, and he listened without comment. He flicked his soft ears, looking at me with intelligent brown eyes. He pushed his velvet nose into my neck letting me know he cared. He was my best friend. I could make him whatever I needed, and I needed someone to listen to the real me.

I sang hymns on his back, sheer volume venting all unspoken feelings. Interspersed were made up songs about beautiful Redwing. All songs accompanied by the musical creak of my saddle. I thoroughly enjoyed being boss over his strength.

After my first year in college, Redwing and I took up our friendship again. It was so much fun to ride him again, but it was harder finding time. One day he nickered at the water trough, but couldn't drink. The vet said he had lockjaw, and needed to be put down.

I went into the granary and sobbed. He had been a faithful friend. I heard footsteps, and quickly dried my eyes. *Nobody is going to see me cry over a horse.* Then I ran to the house so I couldn't hear the shot. When the rendering works truck came I jogged to the backfield and waited for it to leave.

A week later, deep in my heart, I knew college was my first love. Perhaps it was now time to acknowledge that he was no longer 'worth the expense'. His demise was a tiny bit earlier than I was ready for.

That's all.

Thoughts:
- There are many factors in life forming who one becomes.
- I was raised in a big family. What if I was an only child?
- Early on I was introduced to a big God. What if I never heard of God?
- Death is not the end of life. What if I believed my little sister just rotted?
- Forgiveness changed my view of school. What if I hated school all my life?
- I admired missionaries who took risks, and I experienced some control in life with mule Coin and then Redwing. What if I had been born a slave and never had such options?

CHAPTER TWO

GOD SEES AND REMEMBERS

Is This a Calling?

In the year 1943 I read Isaiah 6 where God asks, "Whom shall I send? And who will go for us?" With all my heart I answered as did Isaiah, "Here am I. Send me!" I was sure it was God confirming to me that he was sending me to Africa.

So I declared my interest in going to Africa as a medical missionary. To my surprise nobody, including my Uncles, pooh-poohed the idea. When the High School conducted career interest inventories they assured me that being a medical missionary fit my profile.

I managed to complete High School in three years because I was so eager to get started on my career. Mom created for me beautiful clothes of the latest fashions for college. Daddy paid tuition. A college friend from Church handed me her job working for my board and room. Then, Mom and Daddy drove me across country to Calvin College in Grand Rapids, Michigan, to embark on my calling.

Everything about College fascinated me. Students invited me to join the Mission Club, the Wednesday Bible Study, the Thursday noon Prayer Time, the Science Club, the 'Knighties' 'basketball team, and to teach Sunday school Saturdays in the minority section of town. College equaled excitement. Imagine my shock when I read my first report card. I always had A's in high school, never before a C!

What went wrong? At the library I found a book "How to Study in College". I learned good methods of study, but also learned that all my enjoyable clubs were depriving me of good grades. I changed my ways.

Every chance I got I read about Voltaire, Camas, and Rousseau. If I could figure out how these atheists think maybe I can convince them that God exists and is a "rewarder of those that diligently seek Him" (Hebrews 11:6.) If I can just understand how to argue them into believing I can go back to the streets in Duvall and talk to the men who were so disappointed in God.

I tried out my newly developed arguments on a storekeeper at Christmas time. I had said, 'Merry Christmas', and he had responded, "I'm an atheist. I bah humbug Christmas." All my arguments fell flat. I failed. Now either I still haven't learned the best way to go about this or no argument ever fabricated will convince an atheist.

It took some years before I realized that each of us has assumptions we can't actually prove. The atheist assumes there is no God (maybe because he doesn't want a God) and so he tries to <u>prove</u> there is no God. The Bible tells me "And without faith it is impossible to please God, because anyone who comes to him must believe that he exists and that he rewards those who earnestly seek him." (Hebrews 11:6.) I can't prove God, and the atheist can't disprove Him. Each of us simply has faith in our basic assumptions.

One dream is smashed.

After three years of pre-med I applied to med schools. Each of the five turned me down flat saying, "We are inundated with GI's applying. We will not be taking any women for several years." And I had better grades than some of my GI friends, who med-school admitted right away!

What was the matter with my good God? I felt sure He called me to this career. I asked the head of Foreign Missions if I could serve in Africa right away. He said, "You need to become a teacher or nurse, then we will send you."

So, I interviewed the Nursing School Director. She said, "Yes, you can enter as a freshman. However, none of your pre-med courses will apply because nursing is different."

Shocked I exclaimed, "You mean you will not count any of the courses I've taken in three years of pre-med as applicable to medical nursing?"

She said, "No."

Have I wasted all of high school and college just to ram into a dead end? *God You let me down. I am disappointing Daddy too.* A dark cloud of depression hung over me. I knew it, but didn't care. What is the use of going on? What is the meaning of life if God has not directed me? Why wasn't I content milking cows?

I thought my self-pitying thoughts were justified and not harmful. Until one day as I stood on a bank by a railroad track, I felt an inner impulse to just jump in front of a train. It seemed easy, honest, justified, and hypnotically possible. With sudden insight I knew why people committed suicide. They just stewed in depression and surrendered to despair until, almost without thinking, their bodies just did it. I turned away, conscious now of the horrible consequences of depressive thoughts.

My downer-frame-of-mind wasn't quite all gone yet when I walked past my Chemistry professor's office. Dr, De Vries jumped off his chair and said, "Pearl, come here a minute, and sit down. What is bothering you?" I told him my sad tale, and pent up tears fell unbidden. I was so embarrassed.

He handed me his handkerchief and said, "God doesn't waste education Pearl. I went all through Seminary because my parents wanted me to, and I thought God did too. But when I graduated and faced two sermons a week, plus pastoring a congregation, I knew that would not fulfill me. So I went back to school and became a chemistry professor, which makes me happy everyday. Pearl, when God closes a window, He opens a door."

I wanted to tell him how I admired his unashamed Christian teaching, but not a word got past the lump in my throat. He patted my shoulder and said, "Try to trust God for a better plan, Pearl." I nodded, fled to the bathroom, and sobbed my sorrow over the toilet. I was sure there was no "better plan".

My tuition was paid for. I added psychology courses and managed another major besides biology. I filled in with educational courses, oh so boring. Not even in Africa would I want to be stuck in a class-room. Microbiology! Could they use that in Africa?

Curly blonde hair is a distraction or what?

God brought to the campus a blonde, blue-eyed, curly headed, skinny exchange student from the Netherlands. His very blonde Afro hairstyle made me laugh. We said "Hi" a few times and I thought no more about it until he invited me to a Reformation service. He kept offering me Tums thinking they were peppermints. I didn't have the heart to tell him, so I got thoroughly de-acidified.

Pearl and Rits, 1948

His roommate told him where to go for a haircut. At the salon they had seen his picture in the Grand Rapids Press picturing where he had slept under a tree. He had come at one in the morning from the train station, and the girls in the dorm told him to go away! The salon gave him a haircut and a shave at no cost much to the surprise of his roommate.

I found myself looking for the curly blonde head across campus. When I spied him, my heart skipped a beat or two. It intrigued me to think that the mere sight of a curly blonde head of hair could affect my physical heart. We squeezed out time to walk and talk. One night we were kissing under a dark tree. When I peered over Rits' shoulder I saw a man with his lunch bucket leaning against the wall not an arm's length away, grinning, his teeth gleaming in the darkness. We bolted down the sidewalk, laughing: Rits said, "I bet he was jealous!" What a lovely perception.

Was this friendship part of God organizing a "better plan"? My plans never considered marriage; however I had not factored in the power of hormones. Rits said he wanted to be a missionary to Alaska. And here I was graduating, but not a nurse, nor a teacher, in fact not anything but a generic BA. *God are You leading? How can a person objectively answer that question while feeling like: 'I can't live without this skinny Dutchman'? Alaska is the opposite of Nigeria.*

Seven months passed. I thought: I wonder if this Rits might be God's "better plan". That summer, after Rits had gone to summer school he came out to Washington to visit my family. *How can I introduce this curly-headed-heart-stopper to my family? He can't milk a cow, back up a tractor and trailer, lift a ten-gallon can of milk, weld a broken piece of equipment, or in other words be a farmer's kind of "man".*

But quickly he won their hearts with his genuine interest in their lives. Rits managed to gently tease my inexpressive Mom into expressing herself, and she thoroughly enjoyed him.

The next school year flew by.

My parents said, "Yes".

In the spring Rits called my parents to ask if he could marry me, and we found out my sister Sadie was also planning marriage to Tony in the summer. We had a double wedding. Gathering ivy from the woods and gladiolas, with other flowers, from Mom's garden we gloriously decorated the entire church. Daddy walked down the aisle with one daughter on each side to meet the ones we were marrying. It seemed weird that within an hour we were forever husband and wife.

It was customary there to "steal the bride". Tony and Rits made plans to foil any attempts for anybody to steal their wives even for a few hours. Rits played dumb-Dutchman and told them the cars were up in the hills by Moike.

During the reception some came in late soaking wet from the rain as they searched the hills for our cars. Rits and Tony had put our cars in the garage of a Funeral home, and rented an old Junker-car.

After the reception we asked a friendly couple to put rain-coats over their heads, pretend they were us, and run out to their car. They did a great job spinning their tires for a quick get-away. Many followed them while we slipped quietly out the back door, ducked down in the junker-car, drove the speed limit to Everett, and recouped our cars from the funeral home.

Marriage was more wonderful than I ever dreamed. He loved me, he loved me, and I loved him and accepted my unique Dutchman and his wonderful ways.

We honeymooned on Mt. Rainier, sleeping out under the stars, very romantic. In the middle of the night I heard a scratching sound and grunt noises. I woke Rits and asked him to listen. "Just an animal" he said, and went back to sleep. I lay awake listening to the sounds. I thought: *A bear? The moon is behind a cloud. I can see nothing. Some knight in shining armor I married! I'm sure it's a bear, and we are mighty vulnerable wrapped in a sleeping bag!*

"Honey, I think it's a bear!"

"Just leave him be. Go to sleep."

He did not jump up and protect me. What kind of macho man is this?

Next morning we found the keys were left in the car. I soon admired how he solicited nearby tourists to help him unlock the car. That's my Rits.

We got a small upstairs apartment near Seminary in Grand Rapids, Michigan. Uncle Andy, two years older than me, had also decided to go to seminary, and we invited him to live with us since we had an extra bedroom.

One morning I made a real pancake flop. Rits said, "These are not like my Mom makes!" So I threw one at him like a Frisbee, he ducked and Andy caught it. We used them all as Frisbees and had a great time catching, ducking, and throwing pancakes not fit to eat. We were sitting on orange crates as we hadn't found chairs cheap enough. Two of them were smashed in the fun. The last one collapsed as Rits pulled me down onto his lap for some kissing. But Rits found actual chair-replacements the same day for a dollar a piece.

For five dollars we bought a piano with all brass insides. How we got it up the narrow stairs was a feat. What fun to hear old familiar hymns as Andy played. Rits could also play by ear some really rousing tunes. Married life was one long honeymoon.

After Andy decided to get his own apartment, my sister Sadie came to live with us as her husband Tony was in the army in the Korean conflict. She got a job in Keeler Brass factory, and helped us buy groceries. She was a better piano player than either Andy or Rits, and I could sometimes sing on tune when she was singing too. She could cook like a chef, and we enjoyed not only some improved meals, but also good Chinese checker competition. Many nights we went to bed much too late, because each tried to win the game.

When Tony got back to the states Sadie joined him, and we invited Bob Sutton, also a seminary student, to stay with us. No use letting a bedroom go to waste. I enjoyed the theological discussions we had at the dinner table. It was like I was getting a seminary education, and I loved it. However, he was not as good a sport in Chinese checkers as Sadie was. If he lost several times in a row he would say, "This is a stupid game" and then with a hand mess up all the marbles! Well, it's a small price to pay for interesting theological discussions.

Humpity Dumpity fell off the shelf.

One evening I came home from working at Wurzburg's department store. All day I was thinking about the fun times we were having being married. I was eager to be with Rits, mess up his curly hair, and share his interesting day. I saw him studying by the upstairs window and my heart skipped a beat! In playful fun, I threw a small snowball against the window to draw his attention so I could wave and let him know I was home. I saw him get up and I ran to meet him.

He met me coming up the stairs of our apartment and yelled, "Don't you ever do that again! Don't ever, ever, ever do such a stupid thing again, do you hear me?"

I said, "I just wanted to wave and let you know I was home."

He screamed, "That wasn't funny. I thought it was the Germans. Don't you ever do such a dumb thing again." He was livid.

What kind of wild man did I marry? It isn't like I can run away like I did from a 2x4! I'm stuck. I said very little that night. I didn't know what would send him off. I felt my dream marriage, like humpity-dumpity, had fallen off the wall and I did not know how to put it back together again.

Morning came and Rits acted like nothing had happened, and cheerfully went off to school. The change was bewildering. Nothing more was said. I was afraid to bring it up lest his fury return. Then one day I had set the timer for muffins in the oven. It gave a click before sounding off and Rits came off his chair, eyes flashing anger, "What was that?"

"The timer."

"Don't ever, ever let that thing go off again. I thought it was a German cocking his gun." His face was red with rage. Sure he was in the war. But why was I the target? Why was I being made responsible to moderate or prevent his anger? More put-downs acutely felt were stuffed in that yawning cavern somewhere in my gut. I was acting on the three premises I made under the pump house. Don't confront a man who is angry; run away before you get hurt; and run like blazes if his eyes cloud over.

No more snowballs, no more timers, no more door clicks, no more sneaking up behind to give a kiss. *How many more "no mores" will there be?* I could not understand how a person could flair up in a rage and then ten minutes later pretend like it never happened. I felt confused, stumped, flabbergasted.

Yes, I recognized the fear and felt pity. But why was he taking it out on me, as if I was the cause of his rage? Then I thought: *if I love him enough, avoid the triggers, and forgive each blow-up, he will get over it very quickly.* I meditated on 1Corinthians 13…"Love endures long and is kind; love is not unmannerly; neither is it self-seeking nor irritable, nor does it take account of a suffered wrong." So I figured my part was to love the 1Corinthians 13 way, and I was given by God considerable time to practice this kind of gentle, not irritable, forgiving love!

My agenda behind that love was primarily for it to control his temper, and make life more pleasant for the both of us. I believed my love had that kind of power, just as he believed his anger had power to protect him.

It seemed to me that my love was lots more spiritual than his anger! My three conclusions when hiding under the pump house, made me terrified of confronting him. So his blow-ups were not resolved until years later when I finally understood that war-angers are pure self-protection, and that his love for me was in a separate compartment of his emotions.

Then I did tell him, "I will no longer try to 'fix' your anger. Nothing I say or do helps you with your war fears. I give up. From now on I will calmly say, 'It is your choice. You can be as angry as you decide. But I am going to be happy no matter what you say'."

Money does matter.

To make some income Rits taught two groups of Dutch immigrants English. The Tuesday group of twenty spoke the Groniger dialect, which I struggled hard to comprehend. The Friday group of twenty-three spoke more regular Dutch, but the little I knew was Fries. Rits prepared the lessons; I typed them up, and corrected them afterward. I learned a lot of Dutch this way, and Rits helped me some more by letting me read the Dutch Bible at our meals, helping me with the pronunciations.

We charged twenty-five cents a person for the evening, and fifty cents per couple. The evenings lasted long because Rits designed the lessons to be fun, and both groups were delightful people who desired to learn English fast. Besides we enjoyed the fellowship.

Also Rits had opportunities to preach even in Canada since he could preach Dutch, and that added to our income. The local grocer gave us a big chicken for Thanksgiving, the neighbor gave us potatoes; Dad and Mom gave us canned beef.

I didn't think to worry. I knew God was watching over us!

Yes, I'm pregnant!

Six months had gone by since our wedding. We took for granted that since we wanted a baby it would happen right away. Each of us secretly worried that we couldn't have children, so it was a very joyful day when our pregnancy was confirmed in February.

We went home to the folks in Duvall for the summer and Rits worked on the farm for Uncle Andrew Werkhoven. I helped Mom can fruits and vegetables for the entire family.

We returned to Rits' last year in Seminary with a trailer full of canned meat, canned strawberries, beans and other produce.

October 22 Thelma made her debut. We had her in a basket in our bedroom, and I noticed Rits get up frequently to look at her. I asked, "What are you doing?"

He said, "I was checking if she was breathing. She is. Then I was checking if she was O.K. because she was making funny squeaking noises. Do all babies do that?"

I said, "Yes, they do. Isn't it fun to be a new Daddy?"

A few months later Queen Juliana came to visit Calvin College. When I was walking down the sidewalk with Thelma in a baby buggy Queen Juliana drove by and looked right at Thelma and then smiled at me. I knew she thought Thelma was the prettiest baby she had ever seen!

At the end of Rits' seminary graduation, we moved our little family to Mom and Dad's home. My folks needed me to supervise my brothers while they went to visit my Dad's sister in the Netherlands. Sister Griet had lost her husband and raised her nine children during World War II. Mom and Daddy sent her boxes of things, and now wanted to see how she faired.

Rits had an internship up in Houston, British Columbia as interim pastor for nine weeks

Two weeks into my "job," my creative brothers, fourteen and sixteen, managed to attach gas lawn mower engines onto their bicycles. They were so proud of their accomplishments that they headed for the Puyallup Fair seventy-nine miles south.

They didn't tell me for fear I wouldn't let them go. I found out when there was no one to do their chores! Of course I felt way too responsible, worrying about where they would stay, when they would come back, and what if their "great inventions" stopped working? And how would they call me if they were stuck somewhere in those long stretches of road where there was no phone? I felt angry being responsible-helpless.

I forgot my seeing God was there to help me.

Three days later they came put-putting on the yard, big grins on their faces. They had a great time sleeping with the guys who kept cows and sheep at the fair. They looked at everything, and even went to the Rodeo! They had a problem with a carburetor catching on fire in Seattle, but managed to extinguish the fire with peeing on it.
Rits felt sorry I was handling all this alone and came back three weeks early, which thrilled me plenty.

We nestle into Everson Church.

Since graduation Rits accepted a call to Everson, Washington. Many of the parishioners were farmers. I loved the people and the church activities. Once a month we met with area pastors and wives. The wives gave me preacher-wife advice. "You should not climb cherry trees." (I picked and canned cherries from our tree.) "You should not play horseshoes with the neighbor man. "(He taught me how to make ringers.) "You should not milk cows with a parishioner." (Why not lend a hand?) "You should not win the nail pounding contest on Fourth of July." (It gave me such pleasure to beat the men!)

I said, "Rits, I don't know how to be an acceptable preacher's wife. I'm afraid I'll never fit in."

He said, "True nobility begins when a person ceases to be primarily interested in herself, and begins to ask what God thinks of her. Just be you, Honey. That's plenty good." Good advice, but I still wondered if I 'belonged' being just me.

A 'Northeaster' wind blew huge snowdrifts around our house; we were locked in. I thought, "What fun, no church responsibilities". By ten in the morning we heard the put-put of a John Deere tractor. One of the farmers came "To see if the pastor's family was O.K." By time the three-day storm quit we had had eight farmers on their tractors showing up "to see if pastor and family were O.K". We served coffee and cookies steadily. What great way to enjoy a snowstorm.

Nancy arrived in March of our first year there. A year and three months later Laura arrived. Every Monday and Wednesday we washed flannel diapers and pinned them on a line outside to dry. When it was raining we hung them up in the attic and let a fan blow them dry. What a glorious invention when throw away diapers came on the market. But it didn't come in time to help me.

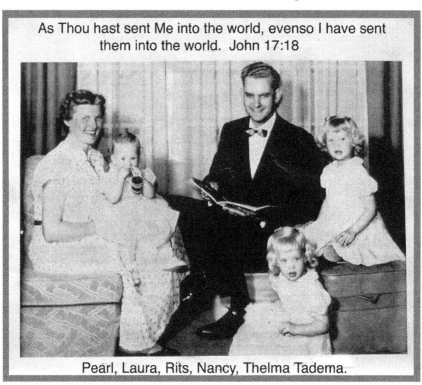

As Thou hast sent Me into the world, evenso I have sent them into the world. John 17:18

Pearl, Laura, Rits, Nancy, Thelma Tadema.

After three years in Everson Church, we were called to be missionaries to Africa. Imagine that! We had three little blonde girls and one baby in my uterus. Our doctor said we were naïve and foolish to take our blonde family into that malaria infested land. But my dream was coming true. And all along I was thinking that my high school 'calling' was crushed forever.

God never forgets.

Everson to Africa

Our doctor did the required physicals and shots, shaking his head.

We had an auction sale of all our goods. Our new washing machine sold for $15.00, but the person who got it needed it. (I have wondered if others knowing their financial limitations just didn't bid.) My folks got the horsehair davenport. (It was later given to sister Sadie, then sister Elaine needed it, then back to us when we moved to Montana, and when we moved to George AFB we had no room so we gave it to our daughter Laura, who gave it back to us when we moved to Carnation.) Our new Chevy Corvair went for half of what it was worth. But we had enough money to buy supplies for Nigeria.

We flew to Holland, Michigan to be officially sent off by our sponsoring congregation. When we got off the plane I saw a whole bunch of people, about 140, pressed against the fence. I thought: We must have some big shots on board. It turned out they were all from the Central Ave Congregation welcoming us as their missionary!

What a fantastic send-off they gave us. Do you know what it feels like to be the center of attention and appreciation while you are already thrilled to be fulfilling your dream?

I'm introduced to Rits' parents.

A train ride to New York and a ship to the Netherlands. There we met Rits' parents. Rits was so excited he couldn't talk Dutch or Fries. He was gone for eight years, and now introduced his wife and three little blonde girls.

Every relative stuffed us with chocolates, cream puffs. apricot liqueur, wines, dried horse beef, smoked eel, raw salt herring, cheeses of all kinds, and for Rits cigars supreme. Many relatives looked like Rits and held their fingers in a triangle just like Rits. Indeed, a wildly wonderful two weeks.

Rits' Mom washed clothes by hand, and taught me how. She cooked on one small kerosene burner, and bought all daily groceries from men who came to the door:
the bread man,
the vegetable man with already washed veggies,
the fish man,
and the milk-buttermilk-pudding-cheese man.
What convenience.
We can't expect that in Nigeria.

Living my dreams in Nigeria.

Soon we were flying to Kano. It had just quit raining and steam literally rose from the tarmac like from a boiling kettle. I quickly took off the children's warm nylon Netherlands clothes and let them run in panties. Big fans like airplane propellers twirled overhead. Thelma tried to catch a huge moth. I said, "They will make your hands dirty, which is not good for a thumb sucker." She turned to the lizards, but they were too quick for her.

Customs took a long time. The wet heat seemed to deprive us of oxygen. But finally we were in our hotel room and taught the children to not ever drink from the faucet, never put their mouths in the bath water, and under no circumstances step on the floor without shoes. Then we put them to bed under the mosquito nets.

The next morning at six a.m. we heard a knock on the door. We were in bed. The waiter walked in holding a tray with tea and crumpets, and cheerfully wished us a great morning! What a superb place Nigeria is ...tea in bed!

We flew on to Jos, where a missionary plane took us to Mkar mission at Gboko. We and our stuff were transferred to the mission carry-all which transported us forty miles further to the Katsina Ala River. There we waited without shade until a barge was available to pole our car and us across.

The sun's rays hurtled down and the quantum light particles piled up on our heads with a distinct heaviness. Eventually our "ferry" was sighted with seventeen oarsmen gliding it to shore. Rits drove the carryall on the barge with all of us in it, and fifteen men pulled the "ferry" upstream with a hemp rope, while two on the ferry pushed it away from the bank with long poles. Then they all jumped aboard, sat in a row on one side and rowed us across to the beat of the song they were singing. I loved this all too short ferry ride.

Missionary Gerard Terpstra met us and we quenched our thirst with tea at their house. Thirty miles more to Zaki Biam, our language school, where the missionaries gave us a great welcome and we settled into our duplex. Pete and Winnie Bulthuis were next to us, having arrived a couple weeks earlier. Winnie complained that her underwear was stolen right off her wash line.

Stepping outside we met a lady with a brand new baby. We stopped to practice the Tiv greeting, "M'sugh." Two-year-old Laura held out her hands to the new baby! The Mom let her hold her, and Laura leaned her cheek on the baby's soft head and kissed her. The Mom said of Laura, "This is a child-of-love." From then on she was known as "Wan-do-ishima', which literally means 'a child with a good-heart.' 'Good heart' is their word for love.

Another lady came up to me, patted my pregnant belly, and then sort of measured it with her hands on either side. This was not comfortable for a stoic Dutch-Frisian lady who had never been touched by a stranger like this before. I didn't want to be offended as she continued to touch with one hand while pointing to the sky with the other. Finally, I realized she was asking me how many moons before the child would be born. I held up one finger, and she responded with delight.

As my new experiences multiplied I came to love and respect these people with their honest, straightforward ways. Watching the women with loads on their heads and smoking their pipes was like stepping into the National Geographic Magazine. Only now I could talk to them (somewhat), hold their babies, and eat their 'ruam' (a white yam pounded like extra stiff mashed potatoes). I loved every minute of being in Nigeria. This dream come true was holding more intrigue than I ever thought possible.

Intense praying goes up for Nancy in Zaki Biam.

We were fully occupied adjusting to the heat and culture, and practicing in the market place our latest lessons from language school. All three girls got dysentery. The nurse claimed the medication would fix it in a week. But Nancy also contracted malaria in spite of all of us taking above average doses of anti-malarials. Rits also suffered from malaria, and lost 30 pounds in three months. I was harshly disillusioned when our best efforts to remain healthy were foiled.

I sponged Nancy with cool water trying to get her fever down. She sat on the pot passing mucous. Then, when she got chills, I held her against my perspiring body: four hours of fever, then four hours of chills.

For three days I could not stop the recurring fevers even though the nurse was giving her all the medication she could take. Nancy no longer wanted to drink. In this tropical climate most children die from dehydration before the disease takes them. I was praying non-stop for God to heal her in His mercy.

To get her to the mission hospital would mean taking her to the river, waiting an unpredictable time for men to bring a barge to pole and paddle us and our car across; and then driving forty miles to Gboko. It would take the better part of a day in the blistering mid-day sun. Can she survive such a trip? *Why don't we have intravenous equipment here?*

It was evening. *No way to get across the river in the dark. We can do nothing until morning.* I worried. I agonized. I felt assailed by circumstances even my prayers could not control. I held Nancy three nights in a row. Her body raged with fever as red blood cells became engorged by the malarial germs, then the cells exploded and her body shivered with chills that my sweating body could not warm. If only there was more I could do*! Oh God, help.*

I went outside on the veranda. There was the Southern Cross; four simple stars hanging above the horizon, standing for salvation. Yet, God seemed even further away than those four blazing suns.

I looked up, and my heart screamed to reach Him somewhere beyond the Milky Way. "Oh God, there is nothing more I can do for Nancy. We've begged You to heal her and she is not healed. However, I guess, yes I guess I should thank You for giving Nancy to us. We've enjoyed your gift for three and a half years. What a pleasure she is. I suppose if You want her back that is Your right. She was Yours to start with. It is after all Your sovereign right. Amen."

I put my head on the cement 'seat' around the edge of the veranda and sobbed: because I was sure that since I had given God permission to take her, He would. Finally, I went back in to lift Nancy's limp body and hold her as long as I could. I pressed her against my chest. She was neither hot nor cold! She opened her eyes and said, "Milk, Mommy?"

I laughed, "With all pleasure, honey".

Very quickly God was wonderfully close to us*: a Daddy who cares and was seeing all along.* Was He waiting for me to relinquish her?

Finally God's gift Aondona comes to us.

And now it was time for our fourth baby to be born. The nurse at the station examined me and said, "The head is down and in place. It is time to go to Lupwe where there's a doctor to help with the birth."

We planned to go the next morning. All night the baby squirmed inside me. When morning dawned the nurse came, and I told her, "It feels like the baby has turned all the way around."

She examined me again and said, "Yes, this child is in the breach position which means he will be born seat first unless we can get to the doctor in time for her to turn the child around again."

As we packed up to leave, labor pains began. We hurried.

The nurse took sterile instruments along in case the child was born on the way. I sat between her and my hubby, Rits, as he drove furiously along the dirt road leading eighty-one miles to Lupwe. The nurse kept repeating, "Please Pearl, don't push. Everything is dust and dirt. Not a receptive place for a new baby."

We hit potholes every fifty feet or so bouncing along like a kangaroo in flight. And at every bounce the baby's head hit my diaphragm, pummeling and bruising it as we bounded along

In navigating a sharp corner the Carryall careened, sending the sterile instruments scooting across the floor, banging into the car's side, and spilling out in the dust. Nurse Neva pleaded with me even more earnestly, "I know it's hard, but please, please don't push Pearl. Just pray that we get there safely, and in time."

I said, "I'm praying Neva. The biggest sharpest pain right now is in my diaphragm where the baby's head bangs every time we hit a hole."

Periodically Neva looked at me with worry saying, "Can you hold out Pearl? We haven't got a single sterile thing!" A couple hours passed, each of us engaged in our own prayer thoughts.

Then, to our relief, thatched roofed huts appeared, and with a tired sigh I walked into the Johanna Veenstra House. Remember, our first missionary to the Jukun? I was given Johanna's bed.

Anita the mid-wife was there and a new doctor from America. "Push Pearl, push hard" they encouraged. I followed their instructions until I felt the walls of the vagina tear with a searing pain. I thought both baby and I were dying. I begged God, "Please give me strength to at least give my child life."

Dr. Joyce said, "It's a boy!"

Her words echoed in my head as "Our son. Our son must be born!" A new rush of adrenalin gave power to push against the ripping pain. Next thing I knew, Rits was kissing my face and saying, "You were so brave. You did it. We have a son, Pearl." I scarce believed we were both alive!

What an incredibly beautiful child. His head and face were perfect, as they didn't have to lead the way through the birth canal. What pure pleasure to hold our nine pound first son. Rits was bawling for joy too. Then Rits took our baby while the doctor stitched up the tears, an event close to the original searing pain, but mercifully not lasting as long. Rits wanted to name him after his father, Cornelius.

I said, "But then he'll be called Corney in school." So we decided Clifford was close enough to honor his dad. It was heaven on earth that evening as we rejoiced over the wonder of our son; feeling him, touching him, kissing all parts of him, thanking God for him, and feeling awesome wonder at a healthy Mom and baby after all.

The next morning, he ran a fever. The doctor examined him thoroughly for any infection. He would not drink. The next day he drank one swallow of water from a bottle. The third day my milk came in. It squirted on his lips, but he ignored it. Our sick boy soon lost two pounds; his wane face was no longer full and pink.

Dr. Joyce said, "I can't figure it out. There is no sign of infection." She called Anita Visser, the midwife.

Anita asked me, "How does his temperature vacillate? How is he acting different from normal? Did you have malaria while carrying him?"

I said, "Yes, I had malaria. He doesn't drink. Four hours fever, four hours chills."

She looked at the doctor and said, "I think this baby has malaria. I've not seen it in a newborn, but he acts like a baby with malaria. Let's give him shots of anti-malarials."

The next day his fever broke, and he began to drink. What an all around relief.

In a few days we made a pleasant trip returning to Zaki Biam. Joyful people greeted us for God had answered the missionaries and the native Christians prayers for our new son and us. We felt warm all over.

Clifford rapidly gained his weight back, and became a husky boy. The native Christians called him 'Jegge Or' meaning 'big man', but we called him 'Aondona' which means 'Gift of God'.

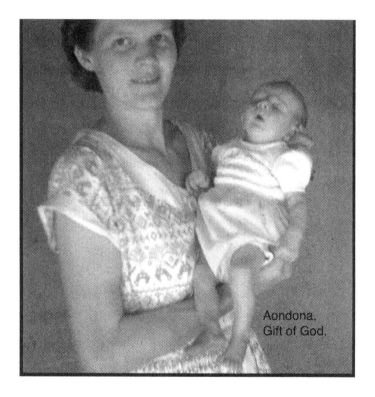

Aondona,
Gift of God.

Thoughts:

- *I paddled hard in college to answer God's call, but He turned my canoe a sharp right. I learned He only turns canoes that are on the move, and He turned it because He knew my heart better than I. I didn't know that deep inside I wanted to be a mother.*

- *I was so awed that He remembered my dream. It was like He was saying, "Oh yes, I remember you saying, 'Here am I send me'. Well, I'm sending you <u>and</u> Rits. I've already arranged the details."*
- *Nigeria was living my dream, but even the best dreams get parasites of difficulty hanging to them.*
- *This ordinary farm girl clung tenaciously to her big, big God.*

CHAPTER THREE

ADVENTURES WITH GOD IN TURAN

Home in Turan at last, 1955

Clifford Aondona was about three weeks old when we were assigned the outpost of Turan as our station. We drove fifty-nine miles to Adikpo where there was a trail leading eighteen miles to Turan. Adikpo was our take off point.

A missionary from South Africa at our station, arranged for us to have fifty-five schoolboys carry head-loads of sixty pounds each into Turan for us. Quite a sight! Six of them carrying our gas washing machine on a rack on their heads, others with loads of flour, sugar, canned meat, chemical toilet, toilet paper, books, sewing machine, bedding, clothes, and sundry other items.

Fifty five school boys carry head loads to our house 18 miles.

I had fixed an orange crate with a canopy of cloth over the top in which to carry our three-week-old Clifford. It was his covered wagon.

When a stalwart man picked him up, put him on his head and turned toward the trail, I wanted to run after him and say, "Don't just balance him on your head, hold him with at least one hand, and please make sure that today you get all the way to Turan."

I frantically stirred my brain for Tiv words. I, speechless, he with a big smile and a proud look strode away with our treasure.

Cliff's covered wagon.

We had a canvas cot, which we turned upside down, and Rits put a bamboo mat over the legs for shade. Laura and Nancy rode like queens in this chariot carried by four men. Rits walked along with them, and they carried all the water we had.

Nancy and Laura in 'hammock' being transported to their new home in Turan, Nigeria.

I took Thelma on the back of our Quickly-motor-bike and assumed we would arrive in a couple hours or so to our new home. (Ten miles an hour on a motorbike seemed reasonable.)A man on a regular bike was assigned to show me the way through the maze of trails. I thought, *I hope he doesn't get too tired trying to stay in front of a motorbike.*

We had our cork helmets on to shield from the sun. The breeze kissed our faces as we motored down the broad trail. It smelled fragrant like dried hay. What a delightful adventure, through savannah grass twelve feet tall. Then the trail dipped down to a stream with tropical vines looking like ropes to swing on. Large trees gave us momentary shade. *It was sure nice of Rits to let me take the motorbike.*

Then quite abruptly the trail narrowed, savannah grass whipped our helmets. We arrived at another little stream and I waded, carrying the motorbike across. The hill on the other side was too steep for the bike and I pushed it up the hill with Thelma trailing behind. After pushing it up the third hill, we stopped to catch our breath, let the sweat evaporate cooling our bodies, and asked our guide, "How far yet?" He pointed his chin up the next hill and said, "Just over that hill!"

Thelma began to cry, "I'm thirsty Mom!"

I said, "I am too. We must get over the next hill." Pushing the bike up the next hill, I heard Thelma whimper behind me. I said, "Honey, please don't waste water crying. I know it's hard." And I felt terrible guilt for not taking a flask of water. Two more hills and we came to a stream of dirty water, which we also forded carrying the bike.

Thelma wanted to drink the water and I yelled, "No. No. It's full of belharsia worms and other things that make us sick. We can't honey, we just can't drink it." She wept and I did 'waste water' too.

Then I had a shocking thought: *if there's a flask of clean water anywhere near, I will fight with my fists anybody to give it to Thelma.* I was horrified at the intensity of feeling…I could violently hurt somebody to get water! Yes, I who loved these people, could actually batter someone for a cup of water!

"My tongue is sticking to the roof of my mouth," I admitted to Thelma.

She said, "Me too. When will we get there?"

"Over the next hill!"

I lost track of how many times our guide said, "Just over that hill". And I lost track of how many hills. The motorbike got heavier with each hill, and my steps got slower.

But five hours after we left Adikpo I saw a big thatched roof providing shade over a mud-brick roomy house, with flowering trees in the front yard. Eric, the missionary we were replacing, had tea ready. We drank over a gallon each. Eric was from South Africa, an Italian Dutch combination making a sturdy body with brown hair and compassionate brown eyes

An hour later that big strapping man used both hands to take Clifford off his head and set him on my lap. I COULD HAVE HUGGED THAT MAN! Instead I thanked him, and grabbed our son, kissing him and showing him off to Eric.

Eric asked him, "Where are the rest?"

He said, "They are resting in a village six miles away, but I knew she would like to see her son so I just came on ahead." What a wonderful man!

In a couple hours Rits and his troop came to increase our joyful reunion. Then the boys came with all the stuff. Eric had his men prepare a lovely chicken dinner, and we then gratefully crawled under our mosquito nets into bed. *Home.*

Our Home In Turan, 1955 to 1958

The next morning we could not see out the windows for all the people who had come to greet us, and welcome us to our home, and to their compound. We belonged to them, and we were safe. I felt intensely happy. This was not exactly living my dream of medical missionary. But here I was with a delightful husband, and four precious children, and I certainly wouldn't trade them for a profession. My heart was bursting with joy.

Next day the cook introduced me to the blind lady. He said," She is very poor. If you want to hire her to peel peanuts for you she would be grateful." I hired her. I sat next to her and peeled peanuts while seeking to communicate in Tiv. She was patient with my efforts, and the children loved her and vied for turns to lead her home.

What about school?

We had a dictionary from Tiv into English, but not from English to Tiv. So when I wanted to tell my cook to beat some eggs to make muffins, I looked up the story in the Tiv New Testament, Acts 22, where Paul was 'beaten.' Using the translated word 'gbweydje' he understood exactly what I meant for him to do with the eggs.

Schoolboys came by after their school to teach me proverbs in Tiv. For instance, 'A bird in the hand is better than ten in the bush', translated was 'A bird in the hand you know!' They were wonderfully persistent in correcting my pronunciation. This was important because a word like "I-YOU" meant house, honey, or body, depending on whether the two syllables were low-high, high-high or high-low.

In the morning, I taught the children kindergarten and first grade from Calvert's Correspondence Course. A father with a very sick lad about two interrupted us, "Do you have medicine for my son?" According to Merck's manual (which we had taken along) he seemed to have Meningitis. I wasn't sure, but gave the lad a big shot of penicillin, plus prayer, and he got better. We were elated to have success with so little knowledge.

Not all interruptions to our "school" had cheerful outcomes. A teenage boy came on his friend's bicycle. His friend said, "Hurry, he was bitten by a viper just a half hour ago. I put a tourniquet above his knee; the bite is in the calf of his leg." I took the only anti-snake venom we had and shot it into him. A viper's bite anti-coagulates the blood, and a person bleeds to death from all orifices in about three days. I hoped the generic anti venom would at least slow it down.

Since the bite was recent, we arranged to have him carried by stretcher the six miles to the Mire Utamen River. Across the river Rits drove him by Rover twenty miles to the Mire Ukirki River. They carried him over the river on the rickety cable "bridge". On the other side Rits took him in the Carryall forty miles to the hospital. We thought if we got him to the hospital quickly enough, they could give him blood transfusions and perhaps save his life.

We waited and prayed three days knowing he got the transfusions. Then we had word by radio that our healthy, strapping young man died anyway. Blood dripped from his eyes and ears, and finally from the pores in his skin.

What more could we have done?

Moses is saved, 1956.

Another day a man and old lady came by with a limp baby about six months old. He had a big starvation belly, tooth pick arms and legs, blue-gray skin with endless bumps from scabies-worms living under his skin, and his eyes stared duly into space. I had grave concern for his life.

The man explained, "This child's mother died in birth. My wife (the mother's sister) took the child and nursed him with our own baby. Our own baby got malaria and died. " (In Nigeria someone else always causes a death.) The mother blamed her sister's baby and refused to feed it. I imagined her breasts leaking milk while this little baby starved!

The man went on, "So we have come to see if you have milk for this baby. I took his grandma along so she could use her breasts as pacifiers until we got here. It has taken us a week. Grandma cannot walk fast. The baby got some water when we squeezed a little from a wet rag into his mouth."

I prepared warm milk in a bottle, but he was too weak to suck. So I took an eyedropper and squirted milk in his mouth, which he swallowed. I thanked God he could still swallow, and got five eyedroppers down him before he was too tired to swallow more. He just let the milk dribble out the corners of his mouth. I encouraged grandma and uncle to go to the native compound and rest.

Every hour I fed him as many eye droppers full as he could take. I called him Moses, since he was rescued from the bush. Finally he could take seven eyedroppers full, and by morning ten. All day I kept this up, periodically trying the bottle, which he refused. All the next night and next day he drank eyedroppers full and, praise God, his eyes began to focus.

That evening, I showed the old grandma how to feed with the eyedropper, and then gave her a bottle with milk. I showed her how to let him suck her breast, then slip her nipple out and the bottle nipple in, and try to fool him into drinking. A big smile was my reward.

I slept like a rock to be awakened about 5 a.m. with the grandma calling my name, "Atesse, Atesse!"

I thought, *Oh no! Moses has died. I should have kept him.* But then I heard a baby cry! I ran outside, and the joy-filled grandma waved an empty bottle and shouted, "Look! He drank it all and wants more!" She fed him bottled milk that day and night. I expected to provide milk and bottles for a year for them. They obviously loved him or they would not have made such a grueling trip.

Next morning they came with Moses, handed him to me, and the man said, "We must go home now. We cannot take Moses home because the village won't accept him. Please take care of him for us."

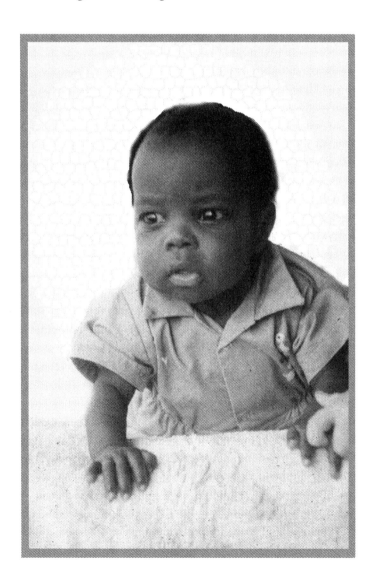

I thought, *Wow. Just like that I'm handed a darling little boy who has already carved out a spot in my heart. Thank you God. What a privilege. I love hugging him and kissing him. It makes him smile*

Rits was on trek with Eric some eighty miles away. What would he think having another child upon his return? I'm sure he'll love him just like the girls and I do.

The next day I covered him with sulfur salve and left it on three days. When I bathed him the third day his scabies were gone! His skin was a nice healthy black. He could sit up now. We all loved our little Moses including Rits of course when he got home.

Akaa quits work.

Oh, oh, one night we hit a snag! Our hired boy, Akaa, who proudly ran our gas washing machine, announced as he was ready to leave work, "I will not wash diapers for Moses! Ugliness tied the knot when he was born. (a Tiv saying meaning too ugly to save.) He is from the Ion tribe. Their ancestors were cannibals and ate my ancestors. It is not right for me to wash his diapers. I quit!"

When he made this announcement I was reading the children a picture Bible story about the Good Samaritan. He saw the vivid picture of the Good Samaritan leaning over the hurt Jew and asked what that picture was all about? I explained the story and added, "The Good Samaritan is like a Christian Tiv person, and the hurt man is like an Ion person. Jesus wants us to help hurt people even if they don't deserve it. That's the Jesus way."

He looked shocked. He had just confessed Jesus as his Savior, and was delighted that he had eternal life. After a long, very long pause he said, "The Jesus way is very hard, very, very hard indeed. See you tomorrow."

I was so relieved he didn't quit, as it was hard to find an intelligent hard worker like Akaa.

Akaa's baby is born.

One day Akaa announced, "My wife is going to have a baby."

I said, "I'm glad for you Akaa. May God give you a healthy baby." How easy it was for me to say those words.

Akaa answered, "My relatives want me to sacrifice a chicken to appease the evil spirits so our baby will be healthy. I told them I was a Christian now, and my God who created the heavens and earth would give me a healthy child. Anyway I am not going to kill a chicken for gods who are no gods. But they beg me daily to not be foolish, but be careful, lest my child die. Don't worry Atesse, I know the true God is real."

Needless to say, I prayed for that baby! When his wife went into labor Akaa ran to tell me, and I ran with him to his hut. The baby was just born, and as I wrapped him in Cliff's receiving blanket my heart stopped at the sight of his squinty eyes, and the layers of fat over his shoulders. Our baby was a Mongoloid! (Down's syndrome)

In my heart I screamed at God, *How could you let this happen to a brand new Christian? He knows I've been praying for a healthy baby. What will he think about praying to you? Is it any better than sacrificing a chicken? Now his relatives will say 'we told you so'!*

Akaa said, "Atesse, he doesn't look right. Do you have medicine to help our baby?"

I said, "Akaa, there is no known medicine for this kind of problem. I am so sorry."

When he came to work the next day I did not know what to say to him. I was mad at God for not protecting His baby Christian and validating Akaa's faith in front of his pagan relatives who now taunted him because he had not sacrificed to appease the evil spirits.

Akaa noticed my dismay, touched my arm, and said, "Atesse, even if all my babies die, I know God is real. I know I am forgiven. I know I will go to heaven. And nobody can take my faith away from me."

Do I, who have known God all my life, have this kind of faith?

Chief Jato Akaa gets the good news, 1956.

We paid our respects to the chief of Turan village. He had sent a goat to welcome us to his area. We learned that we now must give him a gift of equal value to recognize his welcome and to count ourselves as part of the Turan community. We gave him canned meat and candy.

He was rumored to be one hundred years old. I don't know who was counting! We do know that the first missionaries from South Africa knew him. They told him about Jesus the Son of the real God who created the heavens and earth; about Jesus, who came and gave His life that the chief might be forgiven and enjoy eternal life in heaven. He wanted to receive Jesus, but said as chief he had to maintain the idols and sacrifice to appease evil spirits, because that was the way of the Tiv tribe. I don't know if he ever took the step to embrace Jesus-only as the way to Life eternal.

We presented him with the very first copy of the Gospel of John that we had printed so we could distribute them freely. We prayed that he yet decide to receive Jesus' sacrifice.

The missionaries that followed us also did not hear him confess Jesus as his Savior.

CHAPTER FOUR

GOD IS <u>IN</u> OUR HOME SWEET HOME

Strep throat conquered, 1957.

I got a sore throat I couldn't make go away. Then malaria grabbed my run down body. Raw throat, burning fever, and chills tossed me on bed like a wet rag. Rits said, "I'm going to Mkar to get a doctor. Our medicine isn't helping. I'll be back before dark."

Darkness descended pitch black by 6:30 p.m. Why wasn't he back? Did he encounter snakes or tigers in the dark? Did his Quickly motorbike quit on him? Was he stranded without light? I prayed and stewed.

I suppose God in heaven looked down and then looked around for a way to answer my prayers and noticed Eric staying in our guesthouse. He whispered in Eric's ear, "Go to the big house and see how things are."

Eric Casseleggio, a bachelor missionary from South Africa helping us transition to be Nigerian-missionaries walked in. He stood in the doorway of the bedroom as he was not comfortable walking into a woman's bedroom. He asked, "Is there anything I can do for you?"

I said, "Yes, please read the Bible for me and pray that Rits not try to come home in the dark. Akaa and Genyi have taken care of the children and they are in bed."

He opened his Bible and read all of Isaiah 41.

When he got to verse 10 I heard no more. "Fear not, for I am with you; be not dismayed, for I am your God! I will strengthen you, yes, I will help you; yes, I will uphold you with My righteous right hand." (NKJ)

Then Eric got on his knees by a chair near the door and poured out his heart in prayer for us. I was moved to tears by his caring. He said, "I'm going to sleep on your living room floor, so if you need anything at all, just call. I'll be right here."

What a precious brother! The chills robbed me of sleep, so I prayed for Rits. As I looked at the main beam running across the bedroom above the mosquito net, it seemed like it was glowing, and the words sounded in my head, "I am your God. I am taking care of Rits. Fear not. I will strengthen him. Fear not. I will help you." Thank you God for Eric reading Your words.

The next day before noon Rits arrived and said, "Dr. Kok is coming, but preferred walking those six miles." When she arrived, rosy cheeks glowing, she immediately opened her satchel and gave me a big shot of sulfanilamide to cure the strep throat, and then a shot of anti-malarial to douse the malaria. She stayed two days to make sure I was on the mend. What a dear, dear friend. Her tender caring was as healing as the medicine! She was the leprosy doctor, so did some leprosy care, providing pills and shots in nearby villages. She stayed at our guesthouse.

Visitors come via the Adikpo trail.

A young man came running up the trail to our house and informed us, "There are two white men coming on the Adikpo trail. Perhaps one of them is a woman."

We put on tea, dug up peanuts, and prepared yams and chicken for dinner and waited. In due time Harold De Groot and Bill Lemcke appeared. What incredible joy to talk English, know you are understood, and speak about music, philosophy, and world events from an American perspective. Like a drink of cold water in the heat of the day we relished their visit.

They too were told that our home was "just over that hill", and having crested one of the hills they lay down to rest a bit. Harold, pulled his tee shirt up to fan his body. Some natives exclaimed in surprise, "It is a woman!", because he was overweight and had rather large pecks. Others said, "No, it's a man. Look he is dressed in shorts." Women never wear pants, and neither did I to honor them.

After dinner, we sat on the veranda under the stars and ate boiled peanuts. We had prepared two milk buckets full. We talked, laughed, got updated on all the missionaries, shared jokes, and reveled in their presence until early morning. We ate all the peanuts!

Our Coleman lantern burned off to one side over a big dishpan of water. When we turned it off the dishpan was covered with drowned flying ants. Next morning our cook toasted them and enjoyed a tasty snack. (We stuck with peanuts.)

A startling truth is revealed.

Rits had heard over the mission radio that Dr. Van Ieperen would be coming a couple days to enhance our dispensary work. The Doctor did minor operations in open air, pulled infected teeth, and diagnosed illnesses which he said needed hospital attention in Mkar. With determination people could make it to Mkar fifty miles away. That is, if they walked or bicycled the first twenty-six miles. Then they might come across a truck (Lori), which could take them the other thirty-five miles.

The second evening Dr. Len was with us, the dispenser came and asked, "Dr. could you tend this woman who is having her first child? She has been in labor for a long time already."

Dr. Len said, "Pearl, you want to help?"

"Yes, with all pleasure. I'm ready."

He carried the bush lantern and we ducked into the hut. She lay on a bamboo cot, naked, all alone, looking very frightened. I assured her the Doctor would help her. She was not convinced. Each contraction contorted her face as she strained mightily. Half an hour later I asked Dr. Len, "Is she making any progress"?

He said, "Yes, but it will be awhile." He sat on a log with his legs crossed chatting about his six-mile bike trip to our house. He burnt his leg on the exhaust pipe, (as many of us did), carrying the Quickly motorbike across a stream. In two hours of waiting he never ran out of words. However, our young lady, her contractions, and the terror in her eyes distracted me.

As her contractions strengthened and lengthened, I anguished with her. *When is that baby going to come? Is the baby all right? The Doc isn't even listening for the baby's heart beat! She's been in labor for hours already before we came. The poor woman is near exhaustion.* Dr. Len twiddled his thumbs.

Finally, finally and at last, Dr. Len said, "Come here Pearl, you can see the head is coming."

After anther fifteen minutes I said, "Shouldn't the head be further along by now?"

"Relax Pearl. It's her first baby. They always take longer."

He sat relaxed, his little bag at his side, arms crossed in front of him. There was no anesthetic, no sterile environment. She agonized, and I prayed like crazy that her ordeal would soon end. The head eventually crowned and a final-desperate-long push sent her little boy into this world.

Dr. Len said, "Wash him up Pearl, while I wait for the after-birth."

I gave him his first bath, put fragrant baby powder on his little bottom, wrapped him in one of our baby blankets, and then I put his little cheek against mine…. How incredibly soft is newborn skin.

I then presented him to his Mom saying, "You have a very healthy son. He is a fine little man". I took him out of the blanket and laid him on her bare breasts. He immediately nuzzled around looking for a nipple. I covered them both with the blanket.

She smiled. *I love being right here in Nigeria.*

As I stepped outside the hut, the little Southern Cross and the big Milky Way were so bright they seemed like a canopy of protection. I stood still and listened to the symphony of insects, and night birds. I felt like I was in a colossal cathedral. I picked out symphonic instruments as I identified the songs of mosquitoes, crickets, beetles, owls, other night birds, and the drums from the Turan village.

Suddenly it struck me: Jesus, the Creator of all this, was born in a similar hut, except it was for animals. Mary was on a bed of hay, not even a bamboo cot. Joseph spoke words of encouragement, no doubt quoting from the Psalms. Was he feeling helpless to ease the pain? He doubtless did non-stop praying for God to quickly deliver His son.

Did Joseph say, "Mary, I see his black hair! He is almost born!" Then, a long stinging push, and Jesus slips into our world. Did Joseph lay wet Jesus on Mary's bare breasts, while Jesus nuzzled around for Mary's nipple? Did Joseph bury the after-birth? Did he then wrap his son in swaddling linen clothes and lay him in a manger so Mary could get some rest?

Every Christmas we did a nice symbolic manger scene, but tonight I saw how He really came into our lives. The Bible says Jesus and His Father are equal. I wondered: What kind of glory did Jesus have with His Father? What did he leave behind for a bed of hay?

Before I went to my bed I found the answer in Revelations 4. Jesus sat on a throne with rainbow colors all around Him; actually sitting inside a rainbow! The four living creatures were singing, "Holy, holy, holy is the Lord God Almighty, who was, and is, and is to come!" (verse 8) Yes, His glory and His Father's glory were the same.

The twenty-four elders threw their crowns down in front of his throne and shouted, "You are worthy, our Lord and God, to receive glory and honor and power, for you created all things, and by your will they were created and have their being." I imagined Jesus saying, 'Yes, I am the Creator of all, and I am my Father's only son. And now I'm going to earth to become human so I can redeem sinful, rebellious mankind. I am going to make brothers and sisters who will love me down on planet earth.'

Then he stepped off his throne, away from the rainbow colors and across the sea of glass. Heaven was suddenly quiet. Nothing stirred. Angels, creatures, and elders stood aghast. The only sound was his heels clicking on the streets of gold as he left to carry out His mission.

He dropped out of heaven, descended through the galaxies, stepped through the Milky Way, plunged down to a tiny planet called earth, sought out a virgin Jewish girl called Mary and began gestation in her womb. How He did this is a mystery eternity will have to unravel. *"This night I have seen how she gave You birth in a stable, just so we could be saved for eternity. My Lord and my God! I will never, ever will stop loving You!"*

Our Four Children, and then there were Seven.

Clifford.

Now a toddler, Clifford wanted to walk free. All boys under eight years walked barefoot and without clothes. At eight they were circumcised and then wore at least a breech- cloth. I had to tie Clifford's shoes on with many strings so he couldn't take them off. The soil contained "jiggers" which laid eggs under the toenails... an unpleasant business.

Clifford would toddle down the path dropping his shirt, and then stepping out of his shorts: Free as a naked jailbird. In no time at all someone would carry him to me and say, "Atesse, your son is naked!"

This tickled me...and your sons are not naked? But I had to admit there is nothing as naked looking as a little circumcised white boy!

Laura.

From the Turan village a young boy carried a small monkey. Laura reached out to the monkey and it snuggled into her neck like she was its mother. I bought the monkey on the spot.

Laura, now four, dressed her 'monkey-baby' in doll clothes, sang to him, cuddled him, and then pushed him in the dolly stroller. Not wanting to stay 'baby', the monkey leaped out of the stroller, went swinging on the drapes, landed on her shoulder and bounced onto the top of the mosquito net far, far out of her reach. Not any of her cries or calls affected him until he got tired of his game and willingly snuggled into her neck for a rest, knowing, I'm sure, that all was forgiven. When Laura tired of him, he attached to Nancy.

Nancy.

The mischievous monkey sensed Nancy's tender heart. When he was tired, he would pull on her skirts expecting to be picked up. Sometimes she said, "Mom, I don't want to pick him up. He is soo demanding."

I said, "Just say NO real sharp like, and push him away." She didn't have the heart to do this, and I would subsequently see him taking a quick nap in her lap, and then suddenly grab her color crayons and run off.

One day we were all eating peanuts in our 'ate'. (An 'ate' was a grass roof on poles to provide shade.) Nancy had a pile of peanuts in her lap, peeling and munching contentedly. The monkey sneaked up behind her, reached around with his long arm and grabbed a handful. Nancy, now five, gave chase, and the monkey danced just out of her reach! He'd stop, holding his peanuts, and as soon as she reached out to grab him, he hopped away! "Dad," she screamed," Let's sell this rascal!"

When our "cute little monkey" started to bite to get his way we decided he wasn't a good member of our family. Akaa said he would be glad to take the pesky little creature off our hands. We later learned that Akaa's compound had a delightful feast that night!

Thelma.

She was six and a half by now and copied Genyi, our cook, brushing her teeth with a twig from our cashew tree. When I suggested she use her toothbrush, she said, "But look at his teeth, they are whiter than mine!"

She laid her nice dress aside and wrapped a towel around her waist like the blind lady did. When I reminded her she had a dress she said, "I'll save the dress. A towel is much more practical."

She copied the speech of the schoolboys quickly learning the proverbs of their language. And oh how they loved talking with her. And did she ever love her special role with them. She grasped the language better than any of us, and often visited in someone's hut, much to his or her delight. When local visitors came to our compound she intuitively knew who was a thief, or in the case of bargaining who was taking advantage of us. Genyi confirmed that she had it right.

I wondered: *Is it all right for her to go native? Will she forget she is American? I like the way she can relate to the people of our community, but will she later be able to make a transition to an American college with its strange culture?* To avoid this dilemma most missionaries sent their children to a Christian Boarding School in Jos, some 300 miles north on the plateau.

I saw the tears of parents and children as the children boarded the mission plane for Jos. This is not an ideal solution. Wouldn't it be better to teach them at home? Yes, they would absorb the Tiv culture. No, they might not feel comfortable when we go home on leave. What is best for them in the long run?

It was an on-going dilemma.

Moses.

He was now a year and a half and was riding on the hip of Laura, Thelma or Nancy, the biggest part of a day. Genyi also carried him around showing him off to visitors. One of the girls would bath him and then rub his skin with baby oil. He shone like a black light was inside him. Moses was the darling of our house.

We supported an orphan girl, Ikav, so she could go to school and become a nurse. On vacation days she would come home to us, and play with Moses. With all the attention, he scarcely had a chance to learn to walk, but walk he did right into the hearts of our community. That is, the Christian hearts. Others recognized his Ion Tribal features and despised him because his ancestors ate their ancestors, supposedly.

We wanted to adopt Moses so we could take him home to America with us. The government said we needed to get the birth father's signature along with the signature of his compound chief. So we sent a runner to ask the two men to come to our compound to sign the papers for adoption. What did they have to lose? They didn't want him.

When they arrived my heart was full of anticipation. *They must want to sign the papers, otherwise why would they make that long journey?* But when we presented them with papers they shook their heads and said, "No. It is better that he die in the tall grass than go to America and become a slave." We pleaded, Genyi pleaded, Akaa tried his pleas, but they were adamant. They simply turned on their heels and walked back down the trail.

I walked the other way and complained to God. What can we do? What will happen to our precious boy? Do you have another way out? There must be some way to solve this dilemma and keep on loving our little Moses.

There was no way.

M'ember.

One day old, she was brought to our house because her Mom died in giving birth, and no one in the village was nursing at the time. I prepared a bottle and she took to it right away. Her Daddy wanted us to care for her until she could eat food. We knew if we didn't she would die.

She was a gorgeous baby, and so we named her "happiness". The girls played "dolls" with her, carried her on their backs Tiv style, fed her, and pretended they were real Moms.

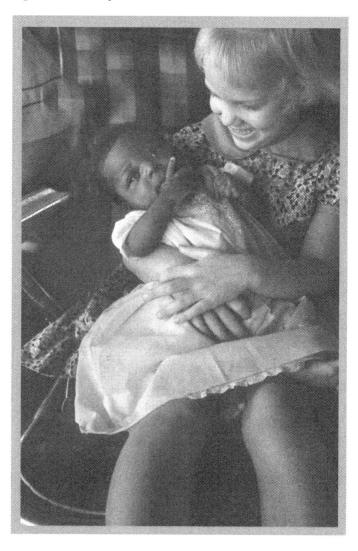

However, she was colicky and cried most nights. I walked the floor with her, let her sleep on my tummy, but nothing calmed the turmoil in her stomach. My most useful remedy was to let her suck on a peppermint wrapped in a handkerchief. But nothing quieted her for long. Three long months went by before she began to live up to her name.

Calvin Rits is almost born.

Our fifth child was a healthy pregnancy. Clifford was incredibly disappointed that he was not going to be black like Moses. Aren't all babies supposed to be black?

To Jos we go. Will we ever find a babysitter?

We decided that for this birth we would go to Jos Hospital, 300 miles north. Our Mission made it mandatory to take a three-week vacation there each year, as it was cooler on the plateau, and provided fellowship with other missionaries. They recognized the value of renewal time.

We were shocked when the missionaries in charge there would not permit us to take Moses and M'ember along!

"They are part of our family! " I proclaimed to Rits, "How can missionaries refuse to let us care for our babies? Would they refuse if their skin was white?" The Miango missionaries would not change their minds, so we had to find someone to care for them while we were gone.

In our search we found a widow lady who was willing to care for Moses, so we got her soap, clothes, food and milk. Since she was poor we included food for her too. Nobody volunteered for M'ember (Happiness). Maybe rumor had gone out about her colicky habits. Anyway we were desperate that last week. So Rits got up in front of Church and called for a volunteer to care for her with gorgeous M'ember (Happiness) in his arms. Nobody stirred.

So he pulled a knife out of his sock and asked, "Well then, who will mercifully end her life? We can't leave her in the house to die of starvation." No response. We were crushed. What could we do? I felt trapped, and I was very angry with the missionaries who refused admission to our black children.

After church, our cook, Genyi, said, "I think there is a lady in my compound who will do it for money."

I said, "Get her quickly, please!" Our dilemma was solved. In fact she liked caring for Happiness because she could dress her in lovely clothes, and had plenty of fragrant soap for herself as well, plus money to spend. She even kept her when we returned.

I took Clifford and Laura on the Quickly and Rits took Nancy, while Genyi pedaled Thelma. We transferred to the Landrover at the Mire U Tamen River, and made another transfer at the Mire U Kirki to the Carryall and so we arrived at Mkar and then flew up to Jos.

Calvin makes his delayed debut.

When I checked in with the mission the doctor, he said, "Since you are at term, let's initiate contractions and have this baby now.

They wheeled me into the delivery room when suddenly all contractions stopped. I cried.

He said, "I'm sorry, we'll have to wait. We have a motel-type room for you here. You can't go back to Miango because the twenty-mile dirt road is rough, plus transportation is iffy. When contractions start there may be no transportation."

Rits caught the next truck back, to be with the children.

I spent three of the loneliest days of my life along those railroad tracks. By the third day I felt desperate and went to the doctor saying, "I can't stay here. I'm taking the next truck to Miango."

I said it with so much conviction and determination that he jumped off his chair and said, "No, no, no. We can't risk that. I'll start the contractions again if you wish."

This time when the delivery room doors opened Rits unexpectedly showed up. The birth was wonderfully uneventful, and Calvin Rits made his debut at seven pounds and twenty-one inches.

The girls expected Calvin to be black too!

Sorry girls, he's white with no hair.

Home is ever the best.

When Calvin was ten days old we flew to Gboko, then took the Carryall to the Mirukirki river, crossed on the swinging bridge, took the land rover twenty miles to the Mirutamen river, and crossed over by canoe. Then I tied Calvin in front of me with a tablecloth, got on the Quickly motorbike with Laura behind and took off down the six-mile trail to home sweet home.

Rits first lined up some fellows to carry sacks of flour, and sugar, plus cans of kerosene and petrol to our place. Then he followed suit with Clifford tied to the front of him and Nancy on behind. Genyi pedaled Thelma home.

When I got there, our friends said, "There's a six foot python coiled around your refrigerator. Watch out."

I looked through the window and saw nothing, so I put the children on the dining room table, and began a search of the house. As I looked under the beds, I thanked God I was not looking for a viper. A six-foot python is a lot easier to see, and more friendly, usually preferring to simply slither away. Apparently that's what he did. We never saw him again. We, including Moses, settled into our routine with great joy

Starving Baby brings sorrow.

The father brought a tiny baby girl to us. He said, "Her mother died at birth. Nobody is nursing at our compound. She hasn't had anything to eat. Can you help?"

She was too weak to suck, but could swallow, so I fed her with an eyedropper. At first she could only swallow two eyedroppers full at a time. Then she was so tired she let the milk run out of her mouth. By noon the next day she was taking four eyedroppers at a time. I had hope.

But then the father came back and took his baby saying, 'I'm taking her back to her compound. She must not die here."

I pleaded, "Look, she is taking four at a time. There is hope!"

But he shook his head and walked away with her, her helpless legs and arms dangling over his arm.

I turned to Genyi pleading, "I think she can live. Why is he doing this?"

Genyi said, "It is a shame for a person to die away from his home. The father has no hope, and therefore must do what he thinks is appropriate."

It took three days before she died. I grieved over a life that I believed could have been saved, if only — if only —

Thelma holds the starving baby girl.

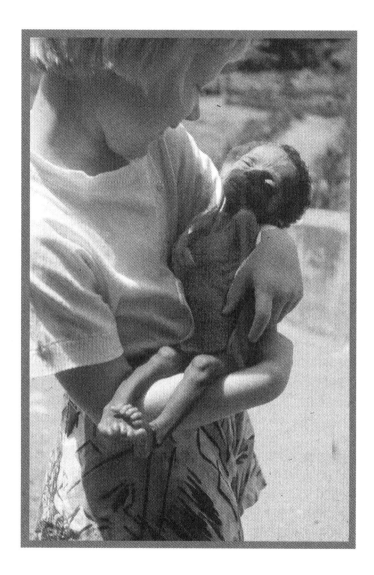

When change is needed.

When I felt like crying for no good reason I knew I needed a change. Not just any change. I needed to touch base with a woman who understood me. So Rits would baby sit and I'd take off on the Quickly motorbike to visit the nearest white missionary woman some twenty miles by trail.

Cruising down the path I felt an urgent need to go to the bathroom. I stopped at some likely looking bushes, and immediately people emerged from all directions out of the tall grass.

I told them "I have to go pee."

Several of them said, "Go ahead", and I realized they expected me to act like them. Women simply partly squat and whenever and wherever the urge arrives they take care of it. (We were crossing in a canoe one day and a man stood up and pee-ed over my shoulder into the river.)

In this case it took some creative thinking for me to communicate that I wanted to do this in secret. Finally one guy understood my intentions and shooed everybody down the trail a bit. He was saying something like, 'I don't get it, but she doesn't want us to watch her pee.'

When I returned from my seclusion, I noticed a man coming down the trail with one hand holding up his very enlarged scrotum. He asked me if I had medicine for this malady. I said, "No, but they can easily fix your problem at the Mkar hospital. Do you know how to get there?"

He said, "Yes, but my wife is sick. Come to my hut and help her first."

I followed him, and ducked into their hut. There was his wife next to a stick driven into the ground. Her hands were tied with a rope so she couldn't leave the stake. She was making weird noises and going up and down against the stake. I felt a huge wave of compassion roll over me. I wanted to take her in my arms and comfort her. As I moved closer she moved away with sheer terror in her eyes. I said, "Why have you got her tied up like that?"

With tears he said, "Because if I don't she gets lost in the tall grass. Please, do you have medicine for my wife?"

Now I was blinking tears back, and said, 'I am so sorry. I do not have medicine for this kind of sickness."

He stood right in front of me, his huge scrotum in one hand, his big brown eyes earnestly searching mine, "Can't your <u>God</u> do anything?"

I was speechless, my heart actually hurt. *What can I say? I have a God who can, but doesn't do that? That wouldn't impress this man who needs a genuine miracle.*

I turned to hide the falling tears, revved up the engine on the Quickly and took off. Then over the roar of the engine I yelled at God as loud as I could scream out the words, "You sent the disciples to say 'the Kingdom of God is at hand,' and empowered them to heal the sick and cast out demons. Of course people believed with that kind of demonstration. Why did You send us here with only words...words this man can't even read. He needs a miracle."

And then I cried: tears for the woman helplessly tied, tears for the man who couldn't find healing for her, tears for the people of this compound who didn't know my God was a God of love and salvation, and tears for helpless me.

And I didn't get an answer!

CHAPTER FIVE

CHILDREN ARE A HERITAGE OF THE LORD

We leave behind part of ourselves. 1958.
Time to go home to America.

We were packing up things to take along when it began to rain. It rained sheets of water and the yard became a shallow lake. The kids loved it. The rivers rose causing some minor bridges to wash out. Six people tried to canoe across the swollen current of the Mire Utamen (where we usually cross) when the canoe capsized. All six were saved, but the canoe was lost.

Then we heard that a mother hippo and her baby had come up the Mire Utamen and devastated Manyam's crops of millet and guinea corn. His compound is where we cross the river! Manyam said, "This hippo is a ferocious Mamma and charges anybody coming within sight of her. She's clumsy looking but has amazing speed. It is extremely dangerous to cross a river with a mother hippo around. They like tipping over canoes."

Of course when it finally quits raining the river will go down and then all hippos will return to the big Katsina Ala River. So we will just stay in Turan until the water goes down, and we can safely canoe across.

In the meantime a mother hen hatched a single chick. Two-year-old Clifford thought it would be nice to hold this baby. Every time he got near the little chick the mother would turn around with feathers sticking out all over and run after Clifford. Was he ever surprised! He bawled her out in an unknown tongue.

As soon as she turned her back he toddled after her baby again. But each time the old hen turned and flew to protect her offspring, and Cliff stopped to yell at her. He kept starting and stopping all over the yard, but it was finally he who got her message.

How many tries before I get God's message?

The Sunday came when Rits had his farewell sermon. Many good-byes were said at Church. Afterwards we sat on our veranda and two old widow ladies came to 'sit a piece' and talk. What better ways to say good-bye than leisurely enjoy each others presence and love? They always vibrated love for their Jesus and that never failed to inspire us.

Then the blind lady arrived saying, "I don't feel right about you leaving without us praying together first." So she led us in a very beautiful, heart-felt prayer for God's care over us. I love these people and will miss their honest, uncomplicated way of caring.

The next morning we were about to leave when around thirty people came by asking us, "What will you give us so we can remember you!" (That would be an endless task!) Then the school children and the Christians gathered in our yard. Rev. Shinyi gave a message from Thessalonians, which amounted to, 'the Christian is in God's care. Let's all pray that God will lead the Tademas to their parents.' Two elders led in stirring prayers. Immediately afterward the old widow ladies burst out in <u>"Blest be the tie that binds our hearts in Christian love. When we asunder part it gives us inward pain, but we shall still be joined in heart and hope to meet again."</u> We shook hands with lumps in our throats and left.

Arriving at Mkar we took our little Moses to the Orphanage there and left him. The caretaker seemed compassionate, but Moses looked oh so lonely. He sensed something unusual was about to happen. His big brown eyes looking at me tore at my heart as I forced myself to walk away. So it was good I had to hurry to the mission plane. There wasn't room for all of us so I went with the three little ones, and Rits drove the Carryall three hundred miles to Jos with Nancy and Thelma. There we would catch a commercial plane.

When Rits finally arrived, someone babysat and we dressed with nylons and tie for an elegant English dinner. Clifford kept rubbing my legs trying to figure out what kind of skin I suddenly had!

Good Ol' USA.

We were only gone three years, so I expected to slip right into the American way. Yes, it was cozy at my folks to hear the cows' moo, the frogs croak, and smell the nostalgic perfume of manure and silage. But it surprised me that I missed the cooing of the pigeons, the village drums, and the sound of mosquitoes, crickets, and owls.

And it seemed impolite to speak a cursory "Hi" in greeting instead of 'U pande iyange dedo ve?' Are you subtracting from this day well? This question followed by: How is your compound? How are your parents? How is your wife? Are your children healthy? There was always plenty of time in Nigeria, and never enough in America. It was good to see friends and relatives again. Adjustment to another culture, though familiar, took about two weeks. One time I even caught myself thinking, *now why is she in Nigeria? Oh no this Bon Marche, Washington.*

During our physicals, the doctor told Rits, "Your pancreas is damaged due probably to starvation in Holland, and now malaria has made it worse. If you want to live long and well you cannot go back to Nigeria."

This was a bigger blow to me than to Rits, because every time he battled malaria he felt like he was not earning his salary. So, for him the thought of feeling energetic and working without illness was very attractive. I wanted to see Moses again, and I loved my role among the Tiv tribe. I fantasized making a trip back, until one day Rits said, "Forget it Pearl. The chances of ever going back are very slim indeed."

Montana: our new home on the range.

Rits was called to pastor the Manhattan Christian Reformed Church in Montana. Dutch immigrant farmers established this church that was now 75 years old. There were one hundred twenty families as members. It was easy to make friends with these thoughtful, caring people who shared their potatoes, wheat, milk, eggs, and Angus beef with us.

Karen arrives as princess.

When I found I was pregnant, one of the ladies invited me to go with her to her doctor and learn how to have a baby by hypnotism without anesthetic. With mirrors I would be able to watch the whole process for a change.

In due time, on a Sunday evening after church, we hurried to the hospital, and the hypnosis worked as I saw Karen Pearl, eight pounds, enter our family. When we took her home, she was thoroughly welcomed by every sibling.

Clifford, four, was so enthralled he jumped and danced all about the house for joy saying, "She's my baby sister, my baby sister! I want to hold her." Her pink little cheeks, sparkling blue eyes, and ready smile made her a darling of the whole congregation. We never lacked for baby sitters.

Daniel's adoption makes him prince.

One day I got a call from a man in Oak Harbor whose wife had died. He said, "We adopted a Korean boy who is now four years old. I can't care for him. Could you adopt him?"

I said, "Yes, yes, but my husband isn't home right now. Could you call us back?"

A week later we decided to call him, but he had already sent the boy back to the Holt Adoption Agency.

They said, "We have many orphans needing homes. We will send you pictures and you can pick out which one you would like to adopt." When we got the pictures I wanted to adopt a dozen. We knew nobody could fill the gap Moses left, but there were so many Korean orphans needing a Mom and Dad. We could offer for one at least, love and belonging to a family.

We picked out the saddest looking little boy, approximately three years old, the same age as Calvin. I said, "Wouldn't it be fun to have twins?" Then we learned we needed home approval, money for plane fare and medical expenses, plus a visa for him. So Karen was two years old when we finally got the news that Daniel Paul would be arriving at Portland on a certain day.

I took the train to Monroe, and Mom and Dad, my sister Sadie, and Aunt Phyllis went along to get Daniel from the airport. We watched for many hours as one hundred and six orphans were handed to their adoptive parents. We wept with joy over each excited couple. I was emotionally wrung out.

One couple, fifty years old, looked at their Korean son and both burst into tears, so overcome they could not walk the last steps to receive their child. Mr. Holt bridged the gap, and stood there smiling as he watched them bond with the child they wanted all their years of marriage.

When no more orphans were coming off the plane my heart stood still. I heard from two families that they had come at an earlier date to get their child but the child got sick and could not fly, so they had to wait half a year for the next plane. I went to Mr. Holt and asked, "Where is our son?"

He said, "I'll look." He came back carrying a tiny boy with a tear-streaked face. Holt explained, "He was sitting in a corner crying. Here is your son!"

And I felt like that fifty-year-old couple! Immediately I loved our little guy and wouldn't trade him for all the gorgeous little girls in their frilly dresses that we saw before him. He felt my love and wouldn't even let me go to the bathroom without him.

By time we got off the train in Manhattan, he knew he belonged, and his siblings treated him like a celebrity. The church family was enamored of this imported little ray of sunshine! They fed him peppermints and even those who had questioned the wisdom of infusing Korean blood into Dutch stock were won over.

Daniel stuffed himself with food, and when he was too full to swallow more, he left his cheeks full; insurance against not having enough. He found a potato in the garage, and carried it in his pocket for a week, but didn't find a need to eat it.

We learned that he had wandered the streets with older boys rummaging through garbage for food, and often fending off dogs who were also hungry. He was terrified of dogs. The police brought our starving little boy to the orphanage three months before we got him.

Rits took him to the lawyer to finalize adoption papers. The lawyer had been in the Korean War and had a picture of him in a fighter jet. When Daniel saw that, he crawled in a corner and froze in panic. The lawyer spoke a few words in Korean, which horribly increased Daniel's terror. Rits had to hold him and reassure him he was safe.

That day his birthday was set on the same day as Calvin, and we had our twins.

One day the children were singing, "Jesus loves me this I know, for the Bible tells me so." So I said to Daniel, "Jesus loves Daniel too, yes, He does."

Daniel jumped off his youth chair and threw himself on the floor saying, "Airplanes come. Many people dead. Trucks. Hospital." He closed his eyes and threw his arms out on the floor like he was dead. Then I realized that since we had talked about Jesus being up in heaven, he was identifying airplanes with Jesus (both being up). I tried to clarify, but it was useless. It bothered me a great deal that He thought Jesus was dropping bombs out of airplanes. I was so helpless to help him.

As it was cold in winter, I made a playhouse for the children in the basement out of old doors. They had fun adding boards and pounding nails all over it. Some days later I was reading Jesus' words in John 14:2 "In My Father's house are many mansions: if it were not so, I would have told you. I go to prepare a place for you." I thought: *Maybe if Daniel knows Jesus is in heaven making a place for him, he will get an upgraded idea of who Jesus really is.* So at breakfast I said to Daniel, "Jesus is making a house for Daniel in heaven".

He said, "With boards?"

I said, "Yes".

He said, "With nails?"

"Yes, with lots of nails"

He said, "A house for Daniel, like our house?"

"Yes, like ours only much, much better and bigger."

He said, "That's good."

Never again did he identify Jesus with airplanes.

Helplessness in surgery becomes an experience in love, 1960.

Shortly after Daniel arrived I was diagnosed with a medical problem, and needed surgery. I memorized a text as assurance that I would get through the operation all right. I kept repeating this verse because I didn't trust the ones cutting on me to not make a mistake while I slept.

"No temptation (trial) has overtaken you except such as is common to mankind (many women have hysterectomies); but God is faithful, who will not allow you to be tempted (tried) beyond what you are able, but with the temptation (trial) will also make the way of escape, that you may be able to bear it." 1 Corinthians 10:13. It comforted me to trust that God was in ultimate control. He was over-seeing the surgeon and me.

Sometime during that operation I saw Jesus' face. His eyes were filled with love as He gazed my way. I thought He must surely be looking at thousands of His people, and I turned to look, but there was no one besides me. I said, "Lord, is all that love for just me?"

His eyes twinkled, and I knew He was saying 'Yes.' But at that same instant I became aware of the time I took a dollar off my uncle's dresser rationalizing that if he wanted it he wouldn't have left it there. Then all the times I lied to Mom to escape punishment. But worst of all, every hateful, judgmental, sinful, hurtful thought lay bare naked, open and exposed to His all seeing eye. I despaired. *He cannot love me now.*

But His eyes danced, and I knew instantly He had erased all my filthy trash. The love sparkled from His eyes again, just for me. I was overwhelmed, awed, and speechless by such undeserved approval from the One who knew all. I wanted to embrace and forever hang on to that acceptance.

I said, "Jesus, can I come to you now?" Poof! He was gone. As I struggled to open my eyes, I saw white, and excitedly thought *maybe this is the portal to heaven.* I felt someone hold my hand, and as I got my eyes all the way open I was shocked to see it was Rits and not Jesus! Yes, I was horribly disappointed at that moment!

My recovery was delayed by a fever. On the second day of recurrent high fevers Rits said, "Maybe its malaria." It took two days for them to find anti-malarials in Alabama and have them sent to our Montana hospital. By then I could scarcely walk.

Rits arranged for me to spend some time recuperating at Widow Hannah's home. She pampered me. *I sure do like this special attention.* We talked and talked about what life was like with her husband and how life changed after his untimely death from a probable blood clot after an appendectomy.

And I told her just about everything you've read so far. To reveal ones heart and be accepted is to feel loved. God used her to fill up the love I needed to feel special. Once the malaria was gone I got strong fast. The kind lady taking care of our children was burned out, and with open arms eagerly welcomed me home.

Harold John's coming completes our family, 1963.

A few months' later two brothers from the church came over for coffee and wanted to talk to Rits and me. They said, "We have wanted to adopt a little Korean as you have, but our wives don't want to. So we were wondering if you wanted to adopt another little boy. If so, we will be glad to pay whatever it costs."

Wowee,! I thought. *Those ladies are missing out on a huge blessing. Don't they realize that children are a blessing from the Lord?*

Rits and I had already talked about getting one more little boy, but we lacked the funds. This was a miracle to us, and we gladly accepted their offer. We picked out a little two year old to match Karen who was two. A second set of twins would be fun.

Mr. Boersema who had sold us a sewing machine, and later got a new Cadillac, offered to drive us to Portland to pick up our little boy. Thelma, Nancy, Rits and I enjoyed his chauffeuring, except that both he and Rits smoked pipes in the front, so we three begged periodic stops to catch some fresh air.

Mr. Holt handed little Harold John (named after the two brothers) to Rits, and there was instant bonding on Rits' part. Harold John still had starvation sores on his legs, and a big starvation belly. Though he had been in the orphanage for six months he hadn't grown at all because he had continual diarrhea. Two years old, and he only weighed twelve pounds, the size of Clifford at six weeks. He showed no signs of wanting to play or walk. He had teeth for a two year old, but acted like a six-month baby. Inside I said: *Little boy, we'll love you with all that is in us.*

Every store was closed that evening, and we desperately needed diapers. Rits even asked the hospital! But each person he urgently talked to, responded with, "I don't have authority to give diapers to you".

Rits said, "Can't you tear up an old sheet"? But of course nobody had authority to hand out a few rags either. Finally Rits said, "I'm going to call a fellow pastor in this Portland area and ask if he could lend us some diapers for our new son."

I said, "I think all his children are in High school. Probably they don't have any." They did have three dozen. It took considerable urging for his wife to finally agree to part with a dozen, temporarily.

Our precious son whimpered night and day like a lost puppy. The children held him, comforted him, walked with him, and sang to him, but he stayed 'lost'. At night he slept on my stomach, and when that did not stop the whimpering we laid him in the crib up against our bed and Rits and I took turns patting his back, so he would not feel abandoned. Or we had him sleep on the pillows above our heads so we could both reach him and let him know he was not alone.

We had no baby-sitting offers for our little gift from God who had endless diarrhea and laments. But we firmly believed that our corporate love would one day break through his loneliness, and he would blossom into a lovely son.

Tacoma calls us to a new mission

In the middle of this adventure we were called to Tacoma to start a new church there. We moved to a rented house, and met Sunday afternoons at 2:00 in a Presbyterian church on D Street. There were about a dozen servicemen stationed at Fort Lewis who attended, plus a few civilians. This was a huge change for Rits who had been preaching to crowds of four hundred four times a Sunday. Now he was preaching to fifteen plus our family, and it made him so nervous he had asthma attacks for a few weeks. We held Sunday school in our various bedrooms.

Harold John continued to cry at night, only now he was stronger and louder. The neighbor next door called Child Protective Services thinking there was some horrible abuse or neglect going on. When CPS called and asked me what was going on I said, "We've adopted a little Korean boy who is still feeling abandoned. I walk the floor with him half the night."

She gave me the neighbor's number, and I explained our dilemma and invited her to come and take a turn to walk and comfort him at night. She was very understanding: but did not take me up on it.

Though he cried at night his diarrhea had stopped except when we went to church.

One night I was rocking him and singing to him. I looked into his eyes, pools of black, just jet blackness, and I wondered; *what is going on in those unreadable eyes? What is he thinking?* I prayed asking God, "How long before he responds? It's been six long months. I know You will heal him, but could You give me a hint when? When will he quit crying?" As I hugged him and kissed his little neck, I felt a sincere commitment, *I'll love you as long as it takes.*

And then he lifted his little hand and touched my cheek. It was his very first response to love. I hugged him and kissed him over and over wiping tears of joy on his flannel pajamas. From that night on he began to blossom into a most loving son.

Starting a Women's Bible Study

In Tacoma, 1965, Rits said, "We need to start a women's Bible study. I'll canvass the neighborhood inviting women and you lead it."

"Not me! I've never done that. It's not what I'm suited for. No thanks."

Rits: "I think a woman is best suited to lead women. I'll help you prepare."

No way. Does he think I don't have enough to do? I'm not a preacher.

The next day I got up early as I often did to read the Bible and make an agenda for the day. I opened the Bible at my marker. What I read was riveting. God was telling Moses to lead the children of Israel, some three million, out of their slavery in Egypt to the Promised Land. Moses had never even led three million sheep: the order seemed preposterous even though the Lord promised miracle on top of miracle.

Moses said to the Lord, "O Lord, I have never been eloquent, neither in the past nor since you have spoken to your servant. I am slow of speech and slow of tongue." Exodus 4:10

So the Lord said to him, "Who has made man's mouth? Or who makes the mute, the deaf, the seeing or the blind? Have not I, the Lord? Now therefore go; I will be with your mouth and will teach you what you shall say." Exodus 4:11-12

"But Moses said, "Oh Lord, please send someone else to do it."

Oh my! Am I saying "no" to God? Is He telling me that He has made my mouth, and will teach me how to lead a Bible study? Dare I not? But I didn't say anything. I really didn't want to.

The next week Rits said, "I have eleven women who want to come to a Bible study. I set it up for next Wednesday at 10:00 a.m. I'll be glad to help you prepare." And help me he did. I could even prepare a sermon on the lesson! I needed that push.

But after some weeks I said, "I think I can do it alone now. The ladies just want the Bible to give us simple, practical, female help with everyday life. We can catch your bigger insights on Sunday."

Bible study was never boring. One day our goat got out, and I threw my Bible down and ran out of the church to catch her. A couple agile ladies ran out too and helped me tie her up again. They said, "We've never been to a Bible study like this before."

One other day I invited one of the ladies to stop by for tea after class. She told me about hearing a voice as she was driving into town for the Bible study. The voice demanded persistently that she run off the road. She said, "I could hardly hold my steering wheel straight. I had a terrible time resisting."

I responded, "I'm relieved you didn't obey that voice. Does it tell you other things?"

She said, "Yes. Like, if you're a good mother you'd take your children swimming, so I take them swimming. Then it says a good mother takes pictures, so I take pictures. If I don't do what it says, it tells me my children would be much better off if I killed myself."

"How long has this voice been telling you what to do?" I asked.

"As far back as I can remember. When I was about two years old it started."

"Is this voice ever a good voice?" I inquired.

She said, "No. Never. It is always suggesting that my family and the world would be better off without me."

I picked up a little New Testament, and asked, "Would you like to live without this voice?"

"Of course! But I never have."

I read, "If God is for us, who can be against us? He who did not spare His own Son, but gave Him up for us all, how shall He not also, along with him, graciously give us all good things?" Romans

8:31-32. If this voice is not good, it is not from God. You belong to God. So we can tell this voice to go away."

She stood up extremely agitated and screamed, "Don't do it. It won't work! I've always had it. It will ruin your faith."

I replied, "It has nothing to do with my faith. It's God's Word. Lord, rid her of this miserable voice, and don't let it ever come back. In Jesus name…"Before I could say Amen she was out the door and gone.

For three months we did not see her. Then we were attending a conference at Warm Beach Conference Grounds and there she was with her husband. She said, "I've been looking for you. I have not heard that voice again. I waited to make sure it was really gone."

"Well, praise the Lord!" *He gave practical, simple, help for us women from the Bible. And He was with my mouth too, just like He promised Moses.*

CHAPTER SIX

GOD MAKES HIMSELF REAL THROUGH MIRACLES

Filled With the Holy Spirit?

I welcomed a visitor after a church service and he bluntly asked me, "Are you filled with the Spirit?"

"I have the Spirit", I replied, "because the Bible says that if we believe Jesus is God's only Son sent to redeem us, we have been given the Spirit of Christ to live inside us. Is that any different from what you're talking about?"

With a smile in the corners of his mouth he replied, "Some people know when they are filled." And he left abruptly. I thought he lacked politeness, but my interest was piqued.

I did a study on all the times in the Bible where it said something about being filled with the Spirit. It seemed always connected with power to talk about Jesus and to do signs and wonders. Signs and wonders? That lady in the Nigerian hut, tied to a stick making weird noises—that image was always hanging like a specter in the back recesses of my mind along with her husband's earnest words, 'Can't your God do anything?' Could my God really do some healing like that in this day and age?

I even fasted three days asking God to show me how to be filled with His Spirit. On the third day I prayed, "God I'm really hungry. Tell me please, how can I be filled with Your Spirit?" Then a clear thought came: you have My Spirit. To be filled you must let Him have you, all of you."

Patti, a member of the Bible study, invited me to go with her to hear Dennis Bennett, an Episcopal priest, teach on being filled with the Spirit. As we took a seat I noticed another Bible Study member who weekly caused me to hustle for creative ways to stop her from pontificating on all sorts of subjects aside from the Bible study. I truly did not want her to know I was needy. But then I thought: *God, I don't want anybody to stop me from receiving all you have to give.*

Father Bennett said, "All who want to receive the fullness of Christ's Spirit may come to kneel at the altar." So I did and was praying as best I could when I felt a hand on my shoulder and the voice of 'that woman' saying, "May I pray with you?" God, You are the Giver. If you could use my words to chase away a bad voice, You could probably use even her. As she prayed warm waves of love flowed over me like a warm shower right straight from God. How I wished I could repeat that experience!

I wasn't real sure what exactly I had received. Well, certainly a small lesson in humility and none judgment! I resumed making school lunches, milking the goat, ironing Rits' white shirts, and finding ways to moderate our Bible study chatterbox with love and respect.

I began reading a book by Brother Lawrence on Practicing the Presence of God. It was fun imagining Jesus walking with me. He did say I will never, never forsake you; and He said, "Lo I am with you always, even to the end of the age." Matthew 28:29. So it is OK to imagine Him constantly with me. I stopped by Patti's house and found her in bed. She said, "I wrenched my knee, and can't put weight on it."

Now, what would You do Jesus standing here? So I asked, "Do you want me to pray for you?"

She said, "Yes."

I imagined Jesus standing with me and I said, "Jesus, please touch her knee and make it well. Amen." She called the next day and said, "I'm walking on it and it doesn't hurt."

Maybe it wasn't hurt that badly! Why does my mind want to minimize what Jesus did? I think I'm scared that people will think my prayer did it and expect me to perform whenever they need something. And I know only Jesus heals, not me. Anyway, she appreciated my concern. So I'll pray and leave all the results to God.

Kindergarten for Karen and Harold, 1965

Karen and Harold started kindergarten, but Harold did not yet speak except for some single words. After the year was over, the kindergarten teacher advised me to let him repeat kindergarten. I said, "No, I think he would learn more if he repeated first grade."

I approached his potential first grade teacher and asked her if he could come to her class, and assured her she needn't give him any special attention. She said, "Yes, send him."

After a month, 1966, I stopped by to see how Harold was doing in her class. She said, "You must not worry about Harold. When he can spell, he can speak. Now, don't you worry!"

Next month I heard from Karen that Harold was going to sing at the Christmas program!! The teacher had asked, "Would anyone like to participate in the Christmas program?" Harold had raised his hand, " I— will— sing."

Then Miss Myers had simply said, "Harold will sing."

I asked Harold, "Will you practice for us?"

He said, "No."

The time for the Christmas program finally came. The lights were dimmed. A spotlight shone on a tiny Korean boy in a white gown with a big red bow under his chin.

Off to the side Miss Meyer's voice said, "Harold John Tadema will sing, 'O Little Town of Bethlehem'." She hit the first note on the piano and Harold's clear sweet voice sang it all the way through while I sobbed into my handkerchief and thanked God the auditorium was dark. *Why in the world do I have to bawl when I am happy?*

About a month later Harold was trying to tell me something. After his third try I said, "Honey, I'm sorry, but I just can't get what you are saying."

He stamped his little foot impatiently and said, "Then—I—will—spell—it! And he did. When Harold could spell, he could also read. He did not need to repeat the first grade!

God, please bless Miss Meyers.

Harold and Karen in first grade.

Tacoma church full of treasures, 1965

On highway 18 we were driving back with our eight children from a visit to my folks in Duvall, when we saw a person walking down the highway with a neck brace and shabby clothes. As we drew closer I said to Rits, "It's a woman! She shouldn't be walking on this highway alone. Let's pick her up and see where she is going."

She squeezed in our station wagon and said, "My car quit. I'm headed for Puyallup." That wasn't much out of our way. I offered to pick her up for our Wednesday Bible Study saying, "We read the Bible and find simple, practical help for us women." She readily accepted. After eighteen miles she asked to be dropped off at the ice cream store in Puyallup.

Wednesday I found her address. *Oh my!* The yard was full of old bricks, stove pipes, cans and buckets, lumber, an old VW bus, car parts, and a medley of other "treasures". When she came out of the house I saw that the yard was just an overflow of even more "treasures" in the house. One man's junk is another man's treasure. I have my own 'treasures' in a shed behind the house with old picture frames, bolts and tools. I think she has more than she can handle! But that's just my opinion of course.

At the Bible study she contributed thoughtful questions to our discussion. I invited her to our home for lunch. After all, the Bible says, "Do not forget to entertain strangers, for by so doing some have unwittingly entertained angels." Hebrews 13:2. She was strange to me, a clean Dutch lady! Her clothes had been among the treasures in her house for a very long time, one sweater covered the holes in the underneath one, and the perennial neck brace I think wasn't clean-able. *Mmmnn, not my picture of an angel, but what if—? At any rate she is no doubt one of God's treasures.*

Rits and I discovered she had a college degree in music, owned part of a silver mine in Idaho, and had an apartment building in Seattle which she had boarded up so it could be preserved.

We invited her to church. She said her VW bus would be running by Sunday. I learned later that her low gear wasn't working so she backed it up the 72nd uphill street for six blocks to get to church — truly a creative woman.

As we were singing in church I heard this gorgeous, angelic soprano voice behind me. It was so astonishing I finally turned my head, and all those lovely notes were spilling out of that soiled neck brace. Why was someone so talented as she living like a bum? This didn't fit any model I was brought up with.

I thought of inviting her to the Christian Women's Club so she could see ways in which others could enjoy her beautiful voice. But the Club catered to upper class women, and I sure would stick out with her along! What would Jesus do? He wasn't ashamed to touch the untouchable leper, or eat with cheaters and sinners. She accepted my invitation, and I am ashamed to say I worried, and then prayed she would look decent and worried some more. But when I picked her up she had obviously taken a shopping trip to Goodwill. She had a nice clean dress, earrings and necklace, her hair was washed and combed with a ribbon in it, no neck brace, and even nylons and dress shoes.

I gasped, "You look stunning." We had a good time, but she could not see herself using her voice for others. After the meeting I said, "God has given you an angelic voice." Then she elaborated on years of voice lessons, and learning the laws of music.

I asked, "Can a person who can't carry a tune learn those laws and stay on tune?

She responded, "Yes indeed, but it takes lots of practice."

"Could you teach me after the Wednesday Bible Study?" She did. I learned to project my voice, run up and down the scale, and finally could hear how it should sound. But I couldn't always make my voice do it.

So she declared an ultimatum: "If you practice two hours a day, I'll continue teaching you and you will learn to hold a tune. But you will never be a great singer." Well I wasn't at all sure that two hours of practice (probably doing the wrong thing part of the time) would result in my minimum goal. So that was the end of my voice lessons.

It was easier and more attainable for me to make huge casseroles and fresh bread on Saturday, so we could invite the church over for lunch on Sunday. Nobody remained a stranger in our church.

After the new building was completed we met for lunch in the church basement, and some of the ladies turned the event into a potluck. The children would gobble their food and go out to play. We had a few goats, a calf, guinea pigs, and rabbits. The boys tried to ride the calf, and held a contest as to who could stay on the longest. Our Billy goat loved to butt, and of course the boys pitted their strength against his, and also tried to ride him. Have you ever smelled the rank, musky, nauseous, skunk-like odor of a Billy goat?

After the potluck we had afternoon church service. The entire church reeked of choking Billy goat stink. So we put Billy in his goat jail until we could sell him!

After the afternoon service we held a forum led by Rits in the basement where anybody could ask questions or make comments about the two services. While questions and comments flew about, coffee and cookies were served. It seemed people felt ownership in their church and the numbers increased. Every new family was one more of God's treasures for our church family to enjoy.

Uncle Sam provides a rude awakening 1968.

Breaking news was that the North Vietnamese captured the South Korean ship, Pueblo. We wondered what that meant. The Reserves called Rits and said, "Your unit is being called into active duty. "Report to Mc Chord Air Force Base tomorrow at 08.00." He kept up church work evenings and weekends. He expected to be released any time.

But after three months, he said, "I can't keep this up." All effort at planning remained topsy-turvy. Then they said six months was projected. Suddenly it was changed to two years, and we were assigned to George Air Force Base in the Mojave Desert, California. Talk about a rude jolt!

We stored things like fruit jars and garden equipment in my Dad's granary, but mice lived there so we had to sell or give away furniture, bedroom sets, and non-essentials like an organ because we were moving into a very small four bedroom triplex.

After moving to George Air Force Base I did substitute teaching to augment our salary, which had been cut in half. But the Base had a swimming pool, tennis courts, and a big wide desert to explore, so our eight children adjusted quickly.

The Base Chaplain's wife and I found women eager to attend a Bible Study. So we proposed to go door to door on Base and invite those who were interested. However, the Base Chaplain said, "That's Chaplains work. I don't want you ladies interfering!"

Here we are trying to augment his work and he tells us to stop. *This is disgusting. This is certainly not like the Tacoma Church where every contribution was appreciated!*

After three weeks the Chaplains still did nothing about the Bible study.

I was attending the Officer's Wives Club and heard a speaker telling us about the extended learning services at the Base. Afterward I marched right straight over to his office, and signed up for two post graduate courses. *Phooey on the Chapel. I know this is not a Christian attitude, but maybe God wants me to try another direction. Indeed He can use circumstances to direct my footsteps.*

Pier transformed.

One day I got a call from Jan, still attending the Tacoma Wednesday Bible Study. Another example of how God directs our circumstances. She said, "My husband is very sick. Remember how we studied in Mark 16:17-18, "these signs shall follow those who believe"...and healing the sick was one of them. Do you still believe that?"

I said, "Yes." *What else can I say? Certainly the Bible can't lie.*

She asked, "Could you come up to Tacoma and pray with my husband? We'll pay your plane ticket. The doctor isn't helping a bit."

I said, "I'll fast and pray for a couple days. God can just as easy heal that way." *I can't heal anybody. I don't know what God wants to do about Pier. This is scary business. What if nothing happens and I've wasted their plane ticket money?*

But after a couple days she called again, "He had a real bad spell last night and thought he was going to die. The doctor was drunk, and wouldn't admit him to the hospital. Please, please, could you come?"

I said, "I'm coming. I'll hop a plane today if possible. At the least I can help you with milking and feeding the cows."

On that plane trip I prayed with non-stop fervor. God will you reach out and heal? I don't want to make a fool of myself. I know healing is no big deal for You. Can I depend on You or am I going to look foolhardy? By time we landed I felt an assurance inside myself that God was planning to be gracious to him.

So I said, "Pier, I believe God wants to heal you, but I don't know how to make this happen. So I suggest we read all the verses we can find in the Bible that talk about praying for healing, and then we do whatever it says."

He said, "Sounds good to me."

The first night we read James 5:16 "Confess your trespasses to one another and pray for one another, that you may be healed. " I said, "I've never done this before, but I can think of three things to confess right now" and I did tell them my besetting sins. We spent the entire evening dredging up bitterness, getting people back, hatred, greed, etc. Then we asked Jesus to forgive us. We all three felt clean and happy.

So, before we went to bed, we asked God to do the other half of that verse and heal Pier. I expected to wake up with him well, but he was not at all well.

I said, "Verse 14 of James 5 says to call for the elders of a church to anoint with oil and pray for healing, but I can't think of any elders who would do that." They couldn't either.

Jan and I went out to do the chores. After breakfast Pier joined us at the table to read, Mark 6:8, Matthew 9:25 where Jesus healed every sickness and disease, Isaiah 53:5 by His stripes we are healed, etc. We read and re-read these verses, and I prayed, "God, when we are reading these verses I believe you are healing Pier, but when I look out the window that certainty evaporates."

It was late afternoon when Pier again read Mark 16:18, "They will lay hands on the sick and they will recover." You haven't done that. Why not?"

"No reason."

"Then please do it."

So Jan and I stood up, laid our hands on his head, and I drew a big breath and said, "Lord God, we're trying to believe. Could You help Pier <u>know</u> that You are healing him."

Right then, it was like electricity hit me on the head and buzzed down my arms. Pier sobbed, "God touched me, God touched me." Jan and I wept for joy. Pier stood up, wandered about the room like he was drunk saying over and over, "God touched me. God touched me."

His face was pale, so I said, "Pier, I suggest you take a nap while Jan and I milk the cows and do the chores. Then we'll have steak." Jan yanked three T-bones out of the freezer. After chores we swept the entire barn, and cleaned the walls and ceiling of the milk house, our energy being boundless. When the steaks were sizzling Jan woke

Pier up, and we celebrated. Pier's stomach had not been able to hold solid food for weeks, but now it loved the T-bone!

I called Rits to tell him the good news. He said, "Go to Dr, Den Dulk in Seattle and have Pier examined as confirmation that he is indeed healed." We did, and the Dr found him in good health. To further celebrate on the way home in their pickup, we each smoked a good Dutch cigar. When I got out of the pickup my head was spinning, I could not walk a straight line.

I said, "Maybe we could better find a prayer meeting to celebrate." So, after milking and feeding cows, I called an Assembly of God church. The janitor answered. I said, "We want to celebrate God healing Pier. Do you have a prayer meeting tonight?"

He said, "Yes. I'll meet you at the basement door at seven exactly." Turned out that he called his wife to come, and we had an impromptu thanksgiving service, which couldn't be improved upon. The janitor told Pier he needed to pray for the fullness of Christ's Spirit. As he did he shook like a tree leaf in the wind. As we were driving home, Pier said, "God touched me again!"

Next morning a lady from that church called. She said, "I heard what God has done for Pier. Could you go to Madigan Hospital and pray for my friend there? Fred has some kind of kidney problem and is very sick."

Pier said, "We will go." And we left immediately. I opened the hospital door and Pier stood their pale, cold sweat on his brow. He said, "I'm claustrophobic. I'll pass out in there."

I said, "Oh God, You got one more thing to do for Pier. Heal this claustrophobia and let him pray for Fred in there." Pier took a deep breath, and soon we were at Fred's bedside. Pier opened the window, so I said, "Pier you better pray for Fred right now!"

I was moved deeply by his prayer, which resonated with the emotional feelings he had when he repeated over and over, "God touched me, God touched me."

The next bed held an elderly man who kept looking at me. I said, "Are you a Christian?"

He said, "Yes, would you pray for me too?" I called Pier and Jan over and we prayed for him too.

The next day I had to fly home, so I said, "Let's call and see how our two guys are doing at Madigan." After waiting for someone to check, the lady said, "They both went home yesterday."

I looked out the airplane window thinking: God comprehends each detail of every life down there. Why do I keep trying to figure Him out? He is incomprehensible. But what I like about Him is that He is powerful in **this** life. Psalms 27:13 "I would have lost heart, unless I had believed that I would see the goodness of the Lord in the land of the living."

I was unprepared for the long-term effect on Pier and Jan's lives. Right away he took an armful of New Testaments to the Farm Auction and shared them with his old buddies. He just had to share how God touched him.

A few years later, he sold his farm, moved to the Netherlands and bought a church and parsonage. He remodeled the church into thirty studio apartments, and took in people from the mental institutions, jail, and homeless shelters. They provided breakfast and dinner and transportation to the doctor when necessary.

I was amazed when we visited and saw Pier gently care for these people with lots of practical common sense. For instance, one lady was depressed and didn't want to get out of bed. Pier brought her food and encouraged her, but next day again she didn't want to get up. Pier took a tape measure and measured her from heel to head. She said, "What are you doing?"

Pier answered matter-of-factly, "I'm measuring you for getting a coffin ready because you will die if you don't get up." She stayed up. Jan always had compassion for people, but I didn't know farmer Pier had these talents. *God You are amazing, and know everything about Your children.*

Back at George Air Force Base, I shared with a few friends what God had done for Pier. I was excited about God doing signs and wonders in our day and age. A Mom asked me to come and pray for her teenage son who had just become a quadriplegic. I went with a friend, but the boy was blaming God for his misfortune, and only when his Mom was in the room did he ask for prayer. We prayed knowing that the boy Jesus raised from the dead didn't have "faith" to be raised either!

When I went back to see how he was doing he said, "I don't believe in God. He ain't never done nothin' for me." Nothing I said changed his mind. I felt helpless and perplexed. I thought, *there must be a key to reaching him. What is it?* I never found a key!

I met a lady by the swimming pool who asked me to pray that her glaucoma would be healed. I stood right there and asked God to touch her eyes and heal her. A couple weeks later I saw her again and she said, "I just got back from my eye doctor. He said, 'Funny, there's no sign of glaucoma!' He healed me Pearl. God healed me. Isn't that wonderful?"

"Yes, it's amazing."

After speaking at a meeting in Chino, some ladies asked me to go with them and pray for a lady who was blind. Her husband had called begging for prayer. As we prayed, one of my partners began commanding the spirit of blindness to leave her. Her little dog became agitated, barked like crazy and then ran helter-skelter outside. The lady had her head turned toward me and said, "I see blue flowers on your dress."

We kept praying and then handed her a songbook, "Here, can you read this?" She read it, then got up and played it on the piano while we sang. What an incredible work of God! I thought of the lady in Nigeria and prayed, "God, can You heal her too?"

Three months later her husband called one of them and said, "My wife has gone back to being blind!"

Lord, did we miss something? Should one of the ladies have kept on visiting her? Or did something happen to her? Does she want to be blind for some reason? What do You want us to learn from this? Should we have spent more time reading the Bible with her? Or is this simply out of our hands?

I felt like God had wound a strong kite string around my wrist and the kite was jerking my feet off the ground. To where was all this pulling me? Lord, I feel so out of control.

Bryon rose to live again.

Rits and I were asked to lead a three-day retreat in Edmonton, Alberta. As I was preparing for my part with the women I prayed Acts 4:29 (NKJ "Now, Lord, look on their threats and grant to Your servants that with all boldness they may speak Your Word," and if You want to do verse 30 "by stretching out your hand to heal and that signs and wonders may be done through the name of Your holy servant Jesus", that's O.K. with me too.

We stayed at the pastor's home. Jan and Henry told us about a Mom and her five daughters who would be coming to some of the meetings. This Mom's only son was lying unconscious for three weeks already in the Foothills Hospital. The Specialists said that because of his extremely high, and long lasting fevers his brain was damaged and they believed if he ever regained consciousness, he would be in a vegetative state.

Accordingly in a church up north, their pastor prayed that he would be taken up to heaven so the family would not be burdened with endless financial debt, nor have to deal with extreme handicaps. Henry's church, on the other hand, was praying for him to be made well, and so were all the Sunday school children.

The mother was in my first meeting and asked me to pray for her only son, eighteen year old. I did right away. Then Rits and I went up to the hospital, stood against his bed and prayed asking God to start His healing in this boy. His body was rigid, eyes closed. I lifted his cold rigid arm and it fell back like the stiff leg of a dead calf. *How do I believe and not doubt?*

We asked the family to meet with us to fulfill the confession required in James 5. After that prayer time together, the mother's voice was poignant, "I buried my husband, and my other son. He is my only son. I want him to live."

Oh Lord Jesus you saw the widow on the way to burying her only son, and You had compassion, stopped the funeral, and raised her son from the dead. Surely You feel the same way about this mother, and will heal her son no matter how sick he is. I couldn't get this mother's face and voice out of my mind. My heart ached for her. Will you heal her son Jesus? Please let me find Your answer in the Bible.

I found it. Jesus said, " Have faith in God. For assuredly, I say to you, whoever says to this mountain, 'Be removed and be cast into the sea', and does not doubt in his heart, but believes that those things he says will be done, he will have whatever he says. Therefore I say to you, whatever things you ask when you pray, believe that you receive them, and you will have them." Mark 22:24-25.

Between teaching sessions I kept on asking Jesus, "Will you heal him?" A clear thought intruded: If you say to him, 'Wake up Bryon in the name of Jesus, I will heal him.'

Lord if that's You, could You say that in an audible voice? *Well, I suppose if I heard a voice out of nowhere I'd think I was hallucinating.*

Then that clear thought again: "What do you have in your hand?"

"A Bible."

Clear thought: 'Isn't that My Word? Written, concrete, right in your hand. What more do you need?"

"Nothing really. But Lord sometimes You heal and sometimes for Your own reasons You don't, and I don't want to look like an idiot commanding him to wake up if nothing happens!"

I told Jan, Henry and Rits about the verse and how it was bugging me to go up and command Bryon to wake up in the name of Jesus. No one offered to go with me.

The last day I told Henry, "Tomorrow we fly out. I have to go up and command Bryon to wake up. I can't stop thinking about it. I want you to go with me."

He said, "Oh my! I have to be sure God wants me there. I know what I'll do! I'll put out a fleece." (a 'fleece' is a test to make sure it is God giving these thoughts.)

I said, "Put out two, so you are sure. What will it be?"

He said, "You prayed with a lady who came from forty miles away. Her husband never lets her go out at night. I want to see her at the meeting tonight." And the second one: a pastor didn't want you here because he doesn't believe in healing for today. I want him to stand up and say the conference was beneficial."

I was hanging up my coat that night at church when "that lady" walked in. I held up one finger to Henry across the room. Towards the end of the meeting Henry asked for testimonies concerning the conference sessions. "That pastor" stood up, and I smiled at Henry.

It was midnight before we were in the hospital elevator. I prayed the boldness prayer in Acts 4, for both of us, and that God would add His healing too. Henry asked the nurse if we could pray with Bryon. She said, "Oh yes. Let me adjust his IV, then you can have forty five minutes with him alone."

Oh thank you, Jesus. We each prayed over Bryon, getting up courage I guess. Then I took a deep breath and said, "Bryon, in the name of Jesus, you can wake up now." Nothing.

I spoke louder, "Bryon, wake up in the name of Jesus!" Nothing.

"Bryon, God is healing you, wake up in the powerful name of Jesus." Nothing.

Lord, I have until eight in the morning before we have to leave for the airport. I'm going to command him to wake up until then, so I am sure I'm doing my part in what You want to do for Bryon and his Mom and sisters.

"Bryon, in Jesus name you can wake up now." Nothing. But laughter bubbled inside me, because I suddenly felt like Jesus was right there with us. "Bryon, Bryon! Jesus is here to wake you up!" His eyelids flickered.

Henry's eyes popped wide open and he yelled, "Bryon wake up!" (He could be heard all down the corridor.) And Bryon opened his eyes wide, looking at Henry. Henry told him the way of salvation, and then interrupted himself, "I got to tell Jan and Rits."

While he was gone, I picked up Bryon's arm and said, "Jesus is helping you hold up your arm Bryon". It dropped dead like the dead calf leg. But I persisted, and the fourth time he held it up.

Just then Henry returned, and said, "Jan suggested I try to get him to hold up his arm", so he lifted Bryon's arm and said, "You can hold up your arm in the name of Jesus, Bryon." And he did. Henry was ecstatic.

To put the next two weeks in a nutshell: Bryon began to talk, then remembered his license plate number, his kindergartner teacher, etc., and in about a week he said, "Look at me preacher", and he dropped his legs to the floor and walked down the hall.

That Sunday Henry asked the congregation to sing "Great is Thy Faithfulness" as Bryon walked down the aisle. The song was a fiasco as sobs of joy were heard. Three years later he visited us at our home. I asked him what had changed for him since he was healed. He said, "I know Jesus as my Friend, and I remember better than I ever did."

God never does the same thing twice, but it is always better than I expect. And the part I play in it is so minimal I wonder why God even bothers with me being part of it all.

La Verne steps out in faith. 1970

At George Air Force Base we were nearing the end of our commitment. Three men came to see us from Fountain Valley Christian Reformed Mission Outreach. They were looking for someone who would be able to 'grow' their beginning church. Having heard about the successful venture in Tacoma, they thought Rits was their man. He warned them that such a growing church included "treasures of God" that did not necessarily fit the expected mould. Since these men were second generation Dutch they might have cultural expectations. "We are eager to adjust", they said.

We moved to a rented house in Westminister, an adjoining city, while a more permanent "parsonage" could be purchased. We were unpacking when the pastor's wife from Alberta to whom I had been writing, called and said, "I want to come down and see if God can do for me what He did for Pier. My doctor has approved if I take an escort, and my friend who has relatives there will fly with me. "

I said, "Sure. When will you come?"

The next week we met them at Los Angeles airport. Her escort was whisked away by relatives, as Laverne shuffled toward us leaning on two canes. I thought: *my God what have I gotten myself into? This is one sick lady.* I did not know just how sick until I learned she was on 29 pills every day, had blood clots in her legs and lungs, had angina heart problems, was overweight, and could barely walk with excessive huffing and puffing.

The next day I managed to get her to the end of Huntington Beach dock for fishing. I asked, "How will your life change when God heals you?"

She said, "I want to raise flowers, hunt huge mushrooms that grow in our hills, and help take care of the handicapped in our community."

She wanted to hear the story of Pier again, and we shared confessions to each other since the fish weren't biting anyway. I was gratified that she was prepared to be well, and could visualize herself without canes and without pills. I planned to fast and pray the next day, and perhaps the following day with Rits go through the Bible verses and pray with her.

That night was prayer meeting at church. I said to Rits, "Why don't you take a separate car to get the kids home, and I will take Laverne to see the ocean, which she is longing to do at night."

So after the meeting Laverne and I went to Huntington Beach. The wind roared over our car carrying salt spray, the waves exploded on the rocks in the moonlight bombarding our senses with explosive power. I talked about the unyielding power of the waves being nothing compared to God's power.

We found the big dipper, little dipper, and Milky Way, and discussed the immensity of the universe, boundless, endless, and colossal. Likewise God's unmerited favor to us humans is limitless, immeasurable, and undeserved.

Laverne said, "Pearl, please pray for me!"

I said, "What do you want me to pray?"

"That He heal me!"

Oh God, You are able to do anything. I hope nothing depends on me tonight!

"Lord God, we have just been talking about how great You are. Healing Laverne is simple for You who created humans in the first place. So please do something for her tonight that will show her you are beginning Your healing process in her life." (And then I spoke a sentence or two in my prayer language, got embarrassed, and quit as we had not talked about that gift.)

Laverne began to cry, and then sob. Not knowing what to do, I took her hand. She cried five minutes, then ten, then fifteen, and I silently listened to the waves smashing noisily against the rocks. Finally she said, "We can go home now. I can't tell you what happened tonight, but I will later." And she continued to weep quietly.

The next morning the kids were off to school so I took my trumpet and played a hymn with the mute on. Thelma was taking lessons, and I tried to keep up with her by additional practicing while she was in school.

Laverne came shuffling out of the bedroom with tears streaming down her face, and said, "Now I want to tell you what happened last night. When you started praying in tongues, heaven was opened and I heard angels singing, and trumpets playing. It was exquisite, ethereal, and flawless. Words can't describe what I heard. That's why I cried. Your playing brought it back like a flood. Please keep on playing."

Me play like an angel? Oh Lord, I guess if You could make her hear such sublime music, You can erase my flaws before she hears them. So I played until my lips were worn out.

Laverne said, "I'm going to walk around the block!"

I said, "I'll get the dishes done while you are gone." I saw her carefully shuffle down the sidewalk without her canes! Forty-five minutes later she was still not back. *Maybe she fell. Maybe I should go after her. I'll just wait until the hour is up.*

Before the hour she walked in, her face glowing like an angel's. I stared at her and said, "What has happened to you Laverne? You look like an angel!"

She said, "I got just around the corner praising God for letting me hear His music last night, and then I felt blood clots leave my legs, slup, slup, slup, slup, just like that. I started to walk and my legs felt light. I can walk Pearl! I can walk! See! You can have my old canes. I don't need them anymore!" And she pranced about the kitchen.

"Wowee! Praise God Laverne. He is something else isn't He?"

She said, "Can we go swim in the ocean?"

"Sure. Let's go! It is February; it could be chilly."

Thelma was home for some reason and we took Laverne to the beach. She laughed uproariously as the first wave knocked us all over. After half an hour Thelma and I shivered on the beach wrapped in towels, our lips, hands and feet all blue. But Laverne was just beyond the last wave floating and singing at the top of her voice in a prayer language. When she came in she was flushed and warm!

124

That evening after supper Rits watched with half open mouth as Laverne played with the kids, chasing them about the house, exuding boundless energy. The pitiful lady coming off the airplane was transformed right before his eyes. We could scarcely keep up with her exuberance.

She called her husband to tell him she was healed. He didn't believe her. She had been in and out of the wheelchair for twenty years. Besides he did not theologically believe that God healed in this day and age.

She worried about it. I said, "When he sees you, surely he can't help but believe you're healed."

That evening she had a recurring thought, "This is just temporary." When I prayed with her at bedtime I said, "This thought is not from God. If it comes back tell it to go to hell in the name of Jesus your Healer."

In the morning she said, "Every time I told it to go away, it went away for an hour, then it was back. So I got mad and said, 'Satan you're a liar.' And I flushed all my pills down the toilet, saying, 'Satan, I'm healed and you can't do anything about it...so there.' Then I slept."

We swam some more, only this time I took a couple thermoses of hot coffee along. She could hardly wait to tell the congregation what God had done for her. The way she waltzed into church that night really needed no further testimony.

All too soon she was back on the plane headed for home in Alberta. She trotted off the aircraft to hug her husband, which blew his theological mind. What was he going to do with a healthy wife when he didn't believe that God healed today? He could go to the doctor in their town and peruse the thick folders on all the physical ailments, clots, heart problems, etc. that were recorded. But instead he categorically stated that she must have been pretending sickness.

She cleaned her house, painted every room, and they became foster parents to a handicapped boy. She wanted to be baptized, and the elders chopped a hole in the creek ice and she was baptized by immersion!

She wrote me, "Pearl, I was so thrilled to be baptized that I didn't feel the cold at all!" When spring came she dug a garden and planted vegetables and flowers. She was unstoppable. People came to her for prayer. She started a Bible study. She did crafts, and wrote up meditations. Other churches called her asking her to tell them what God had done for her.

Her husband resolved his theological dilemma by saying, 'God doesn't heal today. Yet she has changed. So that means she was not sick in the first place." This reasoning put his church elders in a dilemma, and they decided to send them both to the denominational psychiatric institution in Denver, Colorado. Doctors could decide the truth.

Laverne called me from Bethesda Hospital and said, "They want to put me in solitary confinement for three days!"

I said, "You have nothing to fear. Take your Bible and have fun talking to Jesus and listening to Him."

On the fourth day she called me back, "They said that emotionally I was thoroughly healthy." We laughed together, delighted at how God works. But as they were leaving the hospital her husband fell off the sidewalk and broke his arm.

When she told me that sad news I said, "Just love him. He's been in control of an invalid most of his life, and now he has a healthy wife and he didn't even get a chance to choose health for her. Be patient. Only God can help him make the adjustments he needs to." However, all her love and prayers seemed to avail little. His arm kept hurting.

He would not let her pray for it, though she did pray for healing quietly at night.

Eventually he had his hand amputated and wore a prosthesis. He died about seven years later.

CHAPTER SEVEN

CHANGES GOD INITIATES

We adventure into Watts, 1970

I was asked to teach high school Sunday school class. All of the teens were Christians and most from good Christian families. I said, "How many of you would like to practice what you believe rather than concentrate on learning more?" They nodded.

I continued, "I met a pastor in Watts (Los Angeles) who is willing on Saturdays to gather ten children who don't know how to read the Living Bible. How many of you would like to teach reading to one Jr. High child?"

They all raised their hands, so I arranged with the Watts pastor, and piled our station wagon full of my class, and drove an hour to Watts. On the trip we planned the passage we would teach, and one volunteered to dramatize the story in advance of the teaching with flannel graph. It was a roaring success. Our Watts students also learned the Bible was God talking to them personally.

One Saturday our Sunday school girl led her particular student to accept Jesus and both were ecstatic. It was such a high day for us all that we sang every mile back to home.

One day a man was shot across the street from our meeting place. We all found it hard to believe that a pop of a pistol could mean someone was off the face of the earth forever. We continued our teaching every week for about eleven months. No incident was ever aimed at us. I always had my station wagon full of eager teachers.

However, some church leaders complained about Watts being so far, and there being worthwhile projects much nearer. I did not understand this was the first tremor to an imminent earthquake. So instead I simply took them to Fairview Mental Hospital where the non-verbal children resided. It was less than two miles from the church.

We each took a handicapped child outside, sat on the grass and sang to them. Little Bobby scratched, bit and kicked the first time, but after the third time he was jumping up and down to be included in the ones taken out. It was heart breaking to watch them crawl as fast as they could to be included.

One of our girls connected with a cerebral palsy child in a wheel chair, and learned to understand his gibberish! We bought them a pop and a cookie. We saw joy birthed in them, and prayed fervently for healing in their lives. Yes, we did boldly pray.

Then wondered: Lord, what is Your purpose in these handicapped lives? It would be nice to know why their lives are like this. Why don't we see physical and emotional miracles as we pray? We're asking You for answers. But then, in a way it doesn't seem to matter where we go, Jesus, You go with us, and people get happier. It's great to be a Christian, even without all the answers.

The good news is too good not to share.

The pastor at Watts asked if I would join some of his ladies in witnessing door to door. I thought, *This will be good education for me*. I was paired with two vivacious ladies. As we walked down the sidewalk they snagged a young man walking toward us...literally grabbed him by the arm. *Wow! This is aggressive evangelism*. They asked, "Do you know how to get to heaven?"

He answered, "I'm not interested. I'm a Black Panther, and I'm making things better for our people right here."

They said, "But we all need to have eternal life too!"

He said, "I gotta go to my meeting. Let go."

Still hanging on to him, they looked at me, "Pearl, help."

I said, "Sir, what stops you from considering the claims of Jesus Christ?"

He replied, "The church is full of hypocrites. They talk about God's love, but what do they do? Look at the lot of our people here! Its just words."

I said, "You're right about that, but I don't know how to change it right off the bat. However for you, don't let hypocrites stop you from entering heaven. By chance do you have a red letter Bible?"

"Yea."

"Then read all the red words. That's Jesus talking to you personally. He loves you, Black Panther. He died to erase your sins, and He does really and truly want you in His heaven."

"You're going to get a sunstroke Blondie."

"I wouldn't mind a sunstroke if I knew for sure I'd see you in heaven with me and Jesus. There's a prayer in this tract. If you pray that and mean it, I'll see you there. Like my friends here said, it is imperative that you make that decision right now. None of us knows how long we are going to be around."

"I never met anybody like you before, Blondie. I promise I'll read those red words and share them with my buddies. Thanks Blondie. Thanks a lot."

He strode off followed by our prayers. And still, when I think of this incident I pray that I will see him in heaven.

Thelma goes to college.

Thelma started Trinity Christian College in Chicago, but after a few weeks disappeared. I worried that she was in trouble. God says I should dump my cares on Him. But that doesn't fix my failure as a Mom. How can I repair my disastrous parenting when I don't even know what I did wrong? What is Thelma thinking anyway? What did I do to let her down?

We heard from someone we knew in Michigan that they had seen her. Several months later we heard from someone she was in Iowa with a man. Then some relatives had seen her in Washington. To want to help and not be able to is like standing in a manure pit over your boots, unable to move any direction.

Some months later at night about two a.m. Thelma walked into our bedroom. She said, "I'm back here." I jumped out of bed to hug her. She said, "I don't know how to keep from going back there."

I said, "You need to ask God's Holy Spirit to fill you. It's the only way to have power to stay close to God."

We three knelt by our bed. Thelma in jeans and t-shirt, Rits and I in our underwear, and she asked God to fill her with His Spirit. I said, "He is most eager to do this for all His kids. You will notice a difference." Then Rits suggested we catch a couple hours sleep.

I said, "I fixed a bed in the sewing room for you believing you'd come home."

The next morning she said, "Mom, I had a strange experience last night. I was praying to Jesus, and suddenly it was like I was lifted up into a white sphere of light. It was wonderful and safe."

I laughed and said, "I think that's an answer to my prayers. When I prayed for you I imagined putting you on the sea of glass before Jesus' throne expecting Him to bless you and keep you safe. I didn't know how to pray. It was my way of trusting you to His care.

"Now Thelma, I promised to speak at the Mother's Club in a couple weeks. Can I share God's goodness to you?"

She said, "How about I go with you and share myself?"

What a great time we had.

Nancy marries Cal.

Nancy went to Trinity Christian College to explore the possibility of speech therapy as a profession. She met Cal Baker, and after eighteen months they decided to get married. We did all the decorating and food preparation, including wedding pictures, and developing a program for the reception. It was such fun to see it all turn out as planned.

Nancy's little Sunday School girls all had to touch her gown, be kissed, and hugged. It was truly a celebration full of love and informality.

They moved to Phoenix as Cal accepted a teaching position there. Though Phoenix was not the other side of the world, she left a big hole in our family. When I got married I didn't even think about how this affected my Mom and Dad.

Laura experiences a trauma.

Laura took a part time job in an Old People's Home as an aid. On her first day she helped admit an elderly woman who did not want to be dumped off there by her children. (That was her perception.) She was distraught, cried and complained bitterly about her lot in life to Laura. She could not be consoled, and four hours later died. Laura came home traumatized, wondering how her children could be so cruel.

Harold and Dan in Christian school.

Harold and Dan went with the rest of our children to Bellflower Christian School. Some bigger boys teased and shoved Dan around calling him dirty Jap, squint eyes, or HoChiMin. We asked the principle to solve the problem. He did not. So we told Dan, "Next time we give you permission to knock them to the ground. We already told the principle we were giving you permission to do this if he could not solve this discrimination."

He said, "They are bigger."

I said, "Anybody who bullies like they do is a coward. They're cowards Dan. But don't try to scare them or be easy. You have to knock them hard to the ground. We stand behind you." I was infuriated that in a Christian school my son could not even get the cooperation of the principal who obviously had no good principles. I would gladly give those cowards a spanking or two myself.

It took Dan three days to get up the nerve. Then he lit into all three of them, and they turned and ran! They had respect after that and left him alone.

However, Harold with his tender heart could not even get angry. Besides it was his teacher who despised him for being Korean in his Dutch school. So we took him out and placed him in the local public school with his friend from across the street. I guess I'm prejudiced against people who are prejudiced because of color. Do they think they are created by God a notch better?

In the meantime, I finished all courses necessary for a masters in education. But two of my proposals for a thesis were turned down as being too difficult to measure. I was not unhappy about that because my real goal was to get a master in counseling. But the proper courses had not been available at George Air Force Base.

Church life was fun. My Ladies Bible Study was a warm accepting group and we did body surfing at the beach for relaxation and in depth conversations. Rits and I enjoyed our church family. So we were totally unprepared for anything other than living happily ever after.

A Church quake hits us.

It seems three of the original men who started this new church did not like the new enthusiastic Christians becoming Sunday school teachers, deacons and elders. Radical life changes, and prayers for healing made them very uncomfortable. In a letter to the Mission Board they complained that we were not reformed. Whatever Rits tried to do to resolve this dilemma seemed to only make foggy whatever the real issues were. So he suggested they call their own pastor, and he would move on. This they did.

I don't know how gossip gets around in a denomination, but one early morning we had a call from Daddy, "What are you guys up to?"

I said, "We're still in bed."

Daddy said, "Together?"

"Of course."

"Well there are rumors around here of a divorce."

"Not a chance Daddy. Don't worry."

I went to rent some U-haul trucks. They at U-haul said they didn't rent without money up front. I sincerely promised I would not leave without paying them.

The man said, "I don't know why I trust you. Take the trucks. Pay me later." As I walked out the door he called after me, "Be sure you pay before you leave."

Rits flew to the Seattle area to find a place to rent. When he reported finding a place to the Mission Board they said, "We changed our minds. You can be a prison chaplain in New York or serve a mission in Florida. We will not approve your Christian Perspectives Seattle move." What a blow. Well, we've always had a good relationship with the Mission Board so something outside our control happened to sour it.

Rits said, "Goodbye then. God has given me a vision and I am constrained to pursue it." So we were on our own. No money for moving.

My Bible Study had a slumber party at our house. We prayed a bit too. As we said our good-byes next day to the precious friendships in the church, they stuck money into Rits' pockets and in mine. We had enough to pay for the U-haul trucks! This was the beginning of trusting God's friends to provide money so Rits could develop his ministry to professional people.

As Rits was packing up his books, a young man came in and said, "God told me this morning to give you this." He handed Rits an envelope. "Don't open it until I'm gone and thank God, not me." He left and Rits found a check for a thousand dollars in the envelope. We had no idea how much we would need this.

Several years later we met this man and he told us he wrote the check in faith because he did not have what God told him to give. However, when his books were audited they found a thousand dollars that had not been entered. God sees everything.

Moving to Bellevue, Wasington, 1973.

We couldn't find a decent place to rent for our six children, so our brother-in-law, Tony Broers, paid earnest money on buying a house in Bellevue. Rits spent sleepless nights trying to answer the question: How do you make a down payment when you have no money and no assets? The Bank was not friendly. They didn't consider children an asset!

Finally a friend in Tacoma said, "Why don't you ask some of your successful friends to co-sign a note so the Bank can lend you the money." Two farmers from Tacoma gladly did this for us. Imagine, no money, no assets, but we had a purchased house!

We were settled in, and a Home Missionary At Large came to our house. His job was to keep peace in the Churches. He asked me not to teach in the Bellevue Christian Reformed Church, because he did not want the dissension of the Fountain Valley Church to be repeated here.

I did not say as Peter did, 'Whether I should obey God or man, you decide.' No, I was still under my pump house conclusions, 'Don't disagree with someone, flee.' So I meekly said, "The Kingdom of God is plenty big for me to minister elsewhere, if that's what God wants."

I could not and cannot understand the church. It was in the Christian Reformed Church that I learned and believed 2 Timothy 3:16, 17 "All Scripture is given by inspiration of God and is profitable for doctrine, for reproof, for correction, for instruction in righteousness, so that the man of God may be thoroughly equipped for every good work*." If we can't believe what it says, what good is a church?*

I felt like I was in a canoe drifting in the fog of Everett Bay. I didn't belong in Church. I didn't belong to Rits' ministry. He did his best to include me, but his "call" wasn't mine.

Then Thelma, Ken and two children moved up from California to Duvall, only fifteen miles away. I loved baby sitting Ericka and Greg. Their little farm had vine maples to swing in, goats, pigs, geese, chickens, and a pony, plus an interesting old barn. I would make up stories about Yahotee a brave little mouse that lived in that barn. Yahotee barely escaped the barn cat, brought wheat in his mouth to his sister, in the nick of time got under a board to escape a red-tailed hawk, hid in Erica's shoe and was put in her suitcase and ended up at grandmas house, and when I ran out of ideas I'd start a story, get Yahotee in a jam, and then ask them to finish the story. I was amazed at their creative fantasy.

At least I wasn't just drifting.

Laura got married and moved to Canada. Clifford was invited by his coach to return to Bellflower, live with him, and play football his last year of high school. Dan and Cal worked part time, and when not working always had guys over. Harold and Karen also had friends coming over. So I made the most of being a homemaker, enjoying our children and their friends.

There are so many things to do. How come there's an empty spot inside? *Yes, it used to be filled with church activities, but that's over. Get used to it Pearl. It's not like you are twiddling your thumbs!*

Then out of the blue, I was asked to consider being president of a newly organized Women's Aglow Fellowship in Bellevue. I never aspired to such a position, and I was not administrative. Could enthusiasm make up for lack of ability? Is this something God actually wants me to attempt? They emphasize the gifts of the Spirit, so I'm acceptable there. The upshot was that a new and exciting challenge dropped into my lap, and I had to trust God to help me do something I didn't know how to do.

God brought together a diverse, complimentary Board. We met one week to make Board decisions, the next week to learn how to use the gifts of the Spirit, and the next week to pray for the upcoming meeting. Out of this success I was invited to speak all over Washington, and even Alaska and Hawaii. I served four very happy years. I belonged to a cohesive Board, and we made every decision with praying; if it was not unanimous we didn't proceed.

At one Board meeting, our publication chairman was stubborn and would not agree with the rest of us. I was feeling irritated with her as disagreement sharpened. But then our Music Chairman said, "I feel like God wants me to wash our publication chairman's feet." She got up to get a bowl of water, a washcloth and towel. We were all humbled and everybody ended up washing everybody's feet. The issue suddenly wasn't important at all! *Even if I'm right, God doesn't always want me to have my way.*

Each meeting after our guest speaker gave her message we offered an opportunity for ladies to come up for prayer. I began to notice some came every single time, and asked prayer for the same things. That's when I saw a deeper need there than could be met with a cursory prayer. Some of our short prayers brought miracles way beyond the scope of our expectations, but others fell plunk, like a rock tossed up to God and falling back with a klunk. As I prayed about those short-of-the-goal-prayers, God seemed to be urging me to go back to school and get a Masters in counseling. So by taking one or two courses at a time I proceeded in that direction.

Meeting ladies at Aglow from many un-identical churches, I was invited to give an eight-week teaching session in each. As I tried to meet the needs in each place I developed six eight week courses: "The Happy Christian Life", "Using the Gifts of The Spirit", "You and your Motivational Gifts," "Who am I in Christ or (The Wonder of Me,)" "Goal Setting as a Christian", and "Fourteen Steps to Freedom in Christ From Addictions."

We chose prayer partners for the duration of each course. I ran personality profiles and interest inventories to help them realize their strengths, and their prayer partners encouraged them to embark on untried adventures. Not only were these courses fun to do, but also the participants and myself grew emotionally and spiritually; fun all around.

CHAPTER EIGHT

YOU CAN'T STOP GOD FROM BLESSING ME

1978 A Debilitating Surprise.

We were attending Calvin and Julie's wedding in Iowa, June 1, 1978. My shoulders hurt. I found no position that allowed me to sleep. But I was the photographer, and I wanted to see the red-tailed hawk nests Calvin was monitoring for his college class. I found I could transcend pain by focusing on something else. But my focusing on sleep did nothing to transcend the relentless pain at night.

One morning when we were home, I paid full attention to making breakfast, but transcending the pain was impossible. I laid back in bed feeling helpless. The doctor prescribed sixteen aspirin a day, and not being used to any medication I turned into a zombie. After two weeks he got the blood samples back.

He said, "I'm so sorry. You have rheumatoid arthritis. There is no known cure. I'm so sorry. I am recommending you to the best specialist in Seattle. He is on the forefront of treatments for this disease. I want you read, 'From Rose to Briar' by Amy Carmichael. I don't personally understand this, but I've seen people who had chronic diseases develop a deeper, richer life with Jesus than I have ever had or can imagine."

I thought: *Jesus can heal me. What can be richer than that? I've seen Him do bigger things than arthritis. Jesus will heal me.* So I asked for healing at the Aglow meetings, and at various churches.

Cliff and wife Kate told me they were praying and fasting for my healing and wanted me to come to Wyoming to visit them. I did come, and they did wonderfully pray very much like we prayed for Pier. There was no miracle. Not even improvement.

I want to insert here that this phase of life is hard to describe. To be honest and truthful without self-pity and without glossing over pain with super spirituality is not easy. Like me, most people have things happen in their lives, which don't make sense. I don't want to remember the feelings of abandonment, anger, frustration, fear, and the desire to flee. I do want to remember how Jesus brought comfort even when I was feeling picked on. My hope is that my experiences will give someone else a fresh look at their own.

In Women's Aglow Fellowship we believed God was our Healer, and we had many proof texts to substantiate that. One precious friend said, "Pearl, you must have some secret sin that prevents your healing." I prayed earnestly about whatever hidden sins might be in me. Then that clear thought came: *"How can you find something that's secret? I have cleansed you from ALL unrighteousness." Wow God. That's a wonderful relief.*

Another friend said, "You must be harboring resentment, or anger against somebody who has sinned against you." In exasperation I prayed, "Search me O God and know my heart, and see if there be any wicked way in me, and lead me in the way everlasting." Psalm 139:23-24.

I read and re-read Job whose friends said he was sinning otherwise this catastrophe would not have hit him. Yet, we are let-in on the fact that God was permitting it as a test. So God is permitting this pain for purposes I can't figure out.

What would I say if God were asking me the questions he asked Job: "Can you bind the cluster of the Pleiades, or loose the belt of Orion?—Can you lift up your voice to the clouds, that an abundance of water may cover you? Can you send out lightning, that it may go, and say to you, 'Here I am!'"Job 38:31,34-35. Chapters 38-41 are all God's questions, and I answered like Job: "I have heard of

You by the hearing of the ear, but now my eye sees You. Therefore I abhor myself, and repent in dust and ashes." Job 42:5-6. "

Job acknowledged that God was sovereign, and he yielded to God his 'right' to be healed and his "right" to be justified to his friends. It doesn't say how long Job suffered on the ash heap. I relinquished 'my right to be healed according to His promises', as Job did, but I wasn't healed. *Now how are You going to turn that into good Lord?*

I accompanied most of those chapters with slides, illustrating the stars, hippos, crocodiles, sunsets, and animals that God used as illustrations of how impotent Job was to rule the Universe. I then presented them in illustrating a speech on 'God's Ways Are Higher Than Our Ways'. *I better give this speech more than a few times so I can remember Who is in control of my life.*

Finally Job prays for his friends and God gave him twice as much as before. *Well Lord that would be nice.* So I prayed for everybody who had hurt me and blessed them in my prayers. *So now Lord, can You tell me when that 'twice as much' will happen to me?*

I read Paul Brand's book, Pain: The Gift Nobody Wants. In India he began treating leprosy patients. "The horrible disfigurement associated with the disease, we now know, has to do with the numbing of the sensation of pain. People with leprosy lack an internal system to warn them of danger, and they often wear their fingers, hands, and feet down to stumps." He goes on to say, "I regard pain as one of the most remarkable design features of the human body, and if I could choose one gift for leprosy patients, it would be the gift of pain. I also wish people in our culture would cease seeing pain as something to avoid at all costs. If we would, our lives would not only be richer, but our bodies would be healthier." So I gritted my teeth and thanked God for pain, but was it necessary to be so severe, and how could it possibly make life richer?

Augustine in His Confessions said, "What is it, therefore, that goes on within the soul, since it takes greater delight if things that it loves are found or restored to it than if it had always possessed them?" (Christianity Today, January 10, 1994) Yes, I know now for the first time what it is like to not be healthy, and I very much want my health back.

Strange that pain and ecstasy should be bedfellows. Lin Yutang's Chinese formula for happiness he lists thirty supreme pleasures in life. Here are two: "To be dry and thirsty in a hot and dusty land and to feel great drops of rain on my bare skin—ah, is this not happiness! To have an itch in a private part of my body and finally to escape from my friends and go to a hiding place where I can scratch...ah, is this not happiness!"

It seems the idea is to be friendly to my pain, treat it as a gift and then it will lead to greater happiness, at least relief, and maybe ecstasy! I couldn't seem to make it work for me.

I was in the specialist's office when I overheard one patient brag about having had eight operations and she declared, "The doctor is now planning to do my shoulders."

The man next to her stood up, swaggered a bit and crowed, "I've had a hip replaced and a knee replaced; the doc is scheduling my elbow today."

A little wizened lady said with pride, "I've had this disease longer than any of you."

Oh God, their identity is their disease. Please, don't ever let me talk about this disease as if it's the real me. "Christ in me is my only hope of glory." Colossians 1:27

I feel like I somehow got on this arthritic conveyer belt that goes round and round like at the Baggage claim. I want off!

I practiced relaxation therapies to get to sleep. We learned about trigger points and if I couldn't reach them to press for seven seconds, Rits did it for me. He was always trying to be helpful, and when he cupped his hand on my shoulder it sucked the pain right out of it. Unfortunately the pain returned when he fell asleep.

The balls of my feet hurt tremendously. Expensive Orthotics were prescribed, but they only helped about three months. Nancy in Tucson recommended a doctor who would remove the offending toe joints. We went to see him and both Rits and I wept when he said, "You don't need to be in such pain over your feet." He recommended a doctor in Washington, and he did one foot at a time. After healing at least my feet were pain-free.

My wrist fell out of joint often, which hurt and made my hand useless. The doctor solidified the joint, though of course I can't bend it. But at least it doesn't hurt anymore.

To get in and out of a car my hip screamed in excruciating pain. I had a new hip joint put in. I thought *that will take care of that hip*, but the new one fell out of joint three times and an ambulance had to take me to the hospital for anesthetic in order to put it back in place.

The third time I told the doctor, "You have to do something. I am terrified that we will be at some remote rest area, and when I'm pulling up my pants my hip will go out and I will be helpless, pants down, on some cement floor until paramedics can get there." So he replaced it with a better one. At least now my right hip doesn't hurt anymore.

I felt like a bird that had flown into a sliding glass door. It was knocked senseless by the sudden blow. When it attempted to fly to safety it found it had a broken wing. It was vulnerable to cats, dogs and curious children with no way to protect itself. It needed help to mend. And I wanted supernatural help— please God.

I had human help to mend, the best medical care and a family that encouraged me. The combination of drugs kept things down to a dull roar, and made life bearable. However, they could not stop the destruction of joints, (my wing was broken), so eventually I also had to have a knee replaced. I felt like I had no way to protect my body.

Through it all, I could not understand why God would delay His healing. I felt for a moment like God had abandoned me, and I resonated with the Psalmist who says in Psalm 18:6 "In my distress I called upon the Lord; I cried to my God for help. From His temple he heard my voice; my cry came before him, even into his ears." Like Job, I needed to tell God how rotten I felt, so that I could receive His assurance that He was still seeing me and I remained His own.

These thoughts were usually short-lived because I couldn't read the Bible without running into other verses about His tender compassion, "For as the heavens are high above the earth, so great is his mercy for those who fear Him ... As a father pities his children, so the Lord pities those who fear him...But the mercy of the Lord is from everlasting on those who fear him and His righteousness to children's children." Psalm 103:11,13,17.

Psalm 139 became the basis for recognizing the delicate, intricate; weaving God did to create me, and I turned it into a teaching course called The Wonder of Me. He loves me even as I am. He sings a song of joy over me. Zephaniah 3:17. I wrote these verses in large letters and tacked them on the ceiling above my bed. I read them every night without glasses.

And when I woke up those words assured me of His love again. During a sleepless night I pretended my pillow was Jesus' lap, and I shared all my feelings with Him. One night I had a profound insight: I thought *even if my body will no longer do anything for me or Him, I can still love Him and He will consider my life worthwhile!* Now, for a life long workaholic that is a meaningful realization!

With that insight came the understanding that I had been doing good works to prove to Him my thankfulness for salvation. Now I've come to know that God always cares about me even when I'm useless because His Spirit lives inside me, and He cannot disown a part of Himself. The injustices of life and its perplexities will all make sense when I see Him face to face and ask Him the reasons why. Until then I can simply trust His love.

Those thoughts produced a new freedom so I began focusing on teaching, and counseling instead of trying to figure out what God was trying to do with my life. I felt like my life was fairly normal with the help of lots and lots of medications. One question I'll ask when I see Him is: Why eighteen years of this? Am I that hard to teach?

Masters in Counseling equips me.

What a day when the cowl was placed over my head, and the certificate in my hand. It represented a lot of persistence, overcoming fear of failure, and time. And though arthritis slowed me down it didn't stop me!

As I walked across the platform the loud voice of our son Cliff boomed from the balcony, "Way to go MOM." I couldn't have felt prouder, having sons like that.

I hung out my shingle calling my business, 'Creative Christian Counseling.' It wasn't long and I found myself fitting people in at

5:00 a.m. Every session was filled with my praying,'Jesus, how do you want to meet this person's needs'? I always ended a session with asking if the person would like me to pray aloud for them before they left. Only once in twenty years of counseling did a person turn me down!

It was like solving a detective story to sleuth down causes and solutions to people's problems. What delight when God provided the end of suspense with His solutions! To write on these scenarios, and explain what I learned would take a couple volumes.

People were telling me I should write up my Christian methods of counseling so others could benefit. I was starting to feel responsible for doing this when I ran into a book by Neil Anderson called Christ Centered Therapy, and he neatly outlined everything I was doing! Now wasn't that nice of God to take it right out of my hands?

Amsterdam Billy Graham Evangelism Convention provides a new adventure. 1983

We were invited to attend this convention in Amsterdam, Netherlands in July. What an experience—three thousand evangelists from all over the world were represented by their diverse flags flying in the Rei Auditorium. In the opening ceremonies they all came marching down the center aisle flags waving. Something got stuck in my throat and tears fell off my cheeks as I realized that this was God's army, my family. Now when I pray "Thy kingdom come, Thy will be done, on earth as it is in heaven" I see this colorful band of people spread over our planet making this prayer come true.

Represented in the hallways were Bible printing companies, short-term missions organizations, social service helps, tractors and well drilling people eager to help,

language translation helps, and a myriad others eager to assist these valiant scouts for Jesus.

I met a rural evangelist from India and asked him how I could pray for his work there. He told me of feeding orphans, housing widows, preaching in communist villages, and trying to feed the hungry. I asked if sending him Bibles would be helpful and he said "Yes, indeed!"

As I prayed for him later that day I realized that I didn't know anything about his family's needs. So I said, "Lord, I would like to meet him again and ask about his family." The Lord arranged that we went to the same small training group in the afternoon and there he was two-rows up from me. He had two sons and two daughters. His wife cooked for twenty orphans. Five old widows cast out of their homes because they became Christians helped wife Sarah as best they could. The orphans and widows lived in the church.

As I was adding these needs to my prayers I thought: *I forgot to ask him about what he as a person needs.* He was getting plenty of printed helps from here, but maybe there was something else on his heart. So I asked the Lord, "I know there are three thousand people here and without Your help there's not much chance of meeting him again, so could You arrange it?" Sure enough, that night we were sitting in the same balcony section. He said, "I need a buffalo so I can provide milk for my orphans."

Then he said, "I want you to come to India and preach the gospel to my people. You preach, I interpret, God saves." I felt my heart leap at the thought. But then I got realistic.

I said, "I'm half sick with arthritis, it costs a lot of money to fly to India, and I'm just a grandma, but I can pray." Truth is I was not considering it. I wasn't a preacher!

We exchanged addresses so we could keep in touch, and it wasn't long and I got a letter saying the entire church was fasting and praying for my coming to India. Well now I couldn't just erase it from my memory, I had to at least pray about it. The more I prayed the more I felt compelled to go until I said, "Lord, let's make a deal. I'll go if You provide the money for the ticket, which was $3,000.00.

We were at a meeting when a lady came up to me and said, "God wants me to say this to you: 'I have set an open door before you which no man can shut. I know you have little strength, but you have been faithful to observe My Word'. And you know what door is open." Then she was gone. I found the verse in Revelations 3:8. God showed it was indeed a message from Him because bit-by-bit people heard of my deal with the Lord and gave gifts. I was amazed that people would trust me with a job that maybe I couldn't fulfill physically.

But my doctor said, "The day before you leave I'll give you two cortisone shots so you can be as comfortable as possible. So I ordered a ticket. My friend Diane heard about my plans and said, "I feel like God wants me to go with you." I was delighted because she was far more travel-wise than I. She proved to be a marvelous support, and wise in her counsel.

The money came in. I paid for the ticket. Well-wishers saw me off, and tucked a few twenty-dollar bills in my pocket. How I would need that money! Diane had to take different planes, but we were to meet in Hong Kong. I was very glad since she had been there before.

Japan

I looked down at the clouds and marveled that I could be in Japan before night. The song, 'Because He lives I can face tomorrow, because He lives all fear is gone.' Floated and re-floated through my mind. *My body is His temple—He lives in me—no wonder all fear is gone—my skin is His skin.*

Japan was an overnight stop. A taxi to the hotel was very expensive, so I took a bus that drove me to the end of the bus line. It was dark, past midnight. The driver said, "Look", and pointed to a large building about six blocks away, "Hotel". He opened the door and indicated I get out.

So I walked through the dark streets to the hotel with two suitcases, one for Dyva's family and mine. *Lord, my skin is Your skin.* Nice hotel. There were even some snacks in the refrigerator, which I thought was exceptionally nice of them. I was hungry since I missed supper. Imagine my surprise when I was charged a substantial price for my little snack the next morning.

Taking a train back to the airport nobody smiled at me though I smiled at them. Now I know why God said to care about the aliens in your country.

Hong Kong

Tall apartment buildings, like dominoes perched here and there, crowded together but not touching, stretched toward the sky. The tallest was a hotel sixty-six stories high. The Indonesian Bank

Building, pure gold color and round, stood out like a gold nugget in the sand.

Diane and I took a tour boat to see the Bay. Motorboats, junks with sails, sampans propelled with a single oar kept the dirty brown water of the Bay rocking. They were all skilled captains. An old lady could steer between boats so my little finger would get squished in the clearance. She tried to sell a painting for $5.00, but the lady on our boat couldn't buy it because she only had $100.00 bills! I despised my position as a rich onlooker.

I do not know how many thousands live on boats, very poor cramped quarters of about ten feet long and six feet wide. First I thought *well, they have plenty of fish to eat anyway.* But then I noticed deadness in their eyes, an apathy, or hopelessness, or maybe it was anemia. Perhaps the soiled water was making them sick with metal pollutants.

I wish I knew some Christians here that we could visit in one of their boats. I called a number for their Women's Aglow, but each time I got Chinese gibberish and they hung up when I spoke English. Still, I was thrilled to be living what I saw in the National Geographic, but one-weekend was enough of this extremely crowded place. I felt squished.

Hong Kong was only thirty square miles, but had eight million people. All the sidewalks were shoulder-to-shoulder people until two am, and then at 4:30 it all started again. The crush was inescapable. It seemed like continual mayhem to me.

Bankok

I flew to Bangkok, Thailand. Diane would be going later and would meet me there at the hotel. I had to pay twenty dollars Boarding Tax, before they'd let me on. I never heard about such a thing! Thank God He had friends tuck a few of those in my coat pocket.

The taxi to the hotel drove and drove. I wondered if he was taking me elsewhere. I had no Thai words to ask. No high rises here. Five million people and every building needed paint.

The Dusit Hotel was like a colorful bird in the midst of green lush tropical foliage. Sitting in the library I overlooked the pool with cascading waterfalls flanked by red, orange and white bougainvilleas with a plumeria tree wafting its perfume into the open library.

Diane and I just had time for a tour the next day to the floating market. Houses were built on stilts, people spit watermelon seeds out their windows, washed clothes in a bucket and rinsed them in the stream. They bathed, and then washed dishes in the water. Young boys fished with their bamboo poles, then swam with the ducks and splashed each other. The slow moving river was their water source, sewer, food source, and scenic view all in one. Motorboats kept it in gray-green turmoil.

The floating market was just that: a hundred canoes jostling for position, some selling straw hats, silk scarves, leather work, fish, rice, nuts, fruit of all kinds. Some women cooked over a little wok in their canoe and sold ready to eat lunch. Some pushed their canoes together to laugh and gossip. In my opinion this was a great restaurant atmosphere.

I bought a scarf for 100 batj, pop for 20 batj, and for 10 batj I got to hold a heavy python, which had just eaten five chickens, so wasn't interested in eating me. (A batj was ten cents.) We watched a mongoose kill a cobra, then watched a cock fight and wondered which restaurant would serve up the loser.

The next morning I headed for Madras, India, with Diane following on a later flight. I had a four-hour layover in Sri Lanka, but we were not permitted to leave the airport because of a civil war going on.

CHAPTER NINE

GOD IS REAL, REAL TO MY SOUL IN INDIA

Madras, now Chenai, was shocking.

Mayhem described Madras airport. Men pulled at my arms calling "Taxi, taxi, Maam!" Shoulder to shoulder people milled about with no direction like cows in a holding pen. *How do I get outside?* Finally, in a far corner I spied a white woman and waved my excitement to her. She heard from the India Bible League that I was coming, and knew I would not know how to handle the disarrays of an Indian airport. Colleen got me out of there, in her car, and to overnight at her house. We have been in contact ever since. She runs an orphanage of 600 now, medical and food assistance in the slums, education for girls, and a women's sewing class so they can earn some money. Diane arrived a few hours later, and Colleen also rescued her!

The next morning she took us back to walk between our 'guardian angels' into the plane for Vemullipalli where we meet Dyva the evangelist. I pretended like these twenty-four soldiers with their rifles were our guardian angels and even got a smile out of one of them. Sarah and Dyva waved as we descended the steps in Vemulapalli, walked between more 'guardian angels', and embraced Sarah in the tiny terminal in the middle of the fields.

Dyva hired a taxi. The buses were on strike. The country was flat, with sugar cane, potatoes, rice, cauliflower, peppers, cabbage, tomatoes, palm trees, and canals. People were living in small thatched roofed houses, with naked little children in the doorways. The women were gorgeous in their multicolored saris. This land is very fertile, but what I saw as prosperity Dyva just informed me has a horrible flip side.

Dyva explained that rich High Cast Hindu men own all this wonderful land. The workers in the field earn maybe 10-15 rupees a day, but it costs them 20 rupees a day to feed a family of four. Orphans and widows die of starvation. Their self-made thatched-roofed hut ares all they own. They cannot even raise a squash plant because they are not allowed to own any land.

The horn on our taxi screamed continually as we wended our way between ox carts, cows, goats being herded, bicycles, taxi-cycles, trucks, and pedestrians. The blacktop ended, and we turned off on a red dirt road that got bumpier and narrower as we went along. The taxi stopped at a village entrance. People waved, brought out two chairs for Diane and I, put necklaces of flowers around our necks, and presented us with a straw in a coconut so we could be refreshed with coconut milk.

I said, "Praise God. Hallelujah." Their joy at our coming was overwhelming. We learned to say "wan'dana'mula" which means 'thank you', or 'good night', or 'good morning', or 'goodbye'.

By time we got to the next village it was dark, but we got the same rousing welcome. After our coconut milk one old lady came up to me and pressed her face against mine. I responded in kind. Then they all wanted a hug!

Soon the lights of the taxi shone on a square cement church, and a small cement house. Fifteen orphans streamed out of the church singing in English, "There's a welcome here, there's a welcome here, there's a Christian welcome here." Then they went on with "Welcome to Auntie Diane" and "Welcome to Mommy" (my new name).

Dyva's simple home delights us.

Dyva put our stuff in the house, mine in one tiny room, and Diane's in the next small room. There was also a pint-sized living room. I said, "Diane and I can be in the same room. Where will you sleep?"

He said, "We stay in the church. It is settled."

"You are to have one day of rest", Dyva said, "because it is a national holiday for Buddha and the many Hindu gods. People are making pilgrimages to the south, all trains packed. No stores are open, and you can see Hindu's bowing at shrines along the road."

"And behold it is all vanity; their works and pilgrimages are nothing; their molten images are wind and confusion." Isaiah 41:29 (NIV)

Dyva was very proud of the "proper bathroom" he had made for us. It was a cement cubicle in the yard, which had a hole in the cement floor over which we could squat. Sarah would bring us two buckets of water, one warm the other cold for our showers. By rinsing our bodies with cupfuls at a time we could 'shower' in half a bucket.

Sarah scolded Diane saying, "God gives us much water. You use two buckets!" When I finished showering and informed her I had used an entire bucket full she clapped her hands with joy, "That is very good."

We woke up to the creaking squeak of an ox cart and the driver shouting "Haa...kaa...Yii" ,urging the oxen on. The twitter of birds, crowing of roosters, the peep peeping of baby chicks and the caw of crows, mingled with the children singing at their morning devotions. I heard the klunkity, klunk of Naila pumping water, the clatter of pans as the women prepared breakfast and the swish swish of the broom as an orphan swept the ground in front of the house.

Sarah said, "I want to be proud of you. What you are wearing is not good. We go to the market and you buy sari tomorrow. I hire a tailor and he make proper blouse for you." She didn't say so, but I know there are no ready-made blouses for us white giants, and they had to be the special short-exposing-the-mid-riff-type blouse that goes with a sari.

Next day a rickshaw-taxi took us to market. I felt sorry for the boy pedaling; it was so hot. At the market Diane picked out a cotton sari, but both the clerk and Sarah said, "Oh no, no, not good". The clerk said, "Only poor people wear cotton," and she closed the door to that section of cloth! We each picked out three pretty ones. It was so hot Diane hired a taxi to get us back home. We had to learn how to fold pleats and tie our saris, and we both had to preach at eight o'clock.

I talked for half an hour about forgiveness and inviting Jesus to come into our lives. Dyva said, "That is too short. You must keep on preaching." So I talked another twenty minutes about the Holy Spirit and how he came to give us power to live like Jesus, and His presence in us gives us peace, love and joy. Dyva said, "She is tired after such a long trip. She will do longer next time!" In my heart I laughed at his perception, but wondered if I could ever live up to what he wanted! So many cultural expectations to learn!

Then Diane and I handed out New Testaments in their Telegu language. (I had purchased 1,000 from the India Bible League.) I don't know of anything that is more fun. The brown eyes of the poor widows, and school children beamed joy for they could never afford to buy such a treasure.

The next morning I greeted the low caste women as they walked with their little scythes to the fields to work all day. Then I strolled around the edge of the village which was divided in two-.low caste with thatched roofs, round mud walls; and high caste with square cement walls and tile or tin roofs. I greeted a child and he screamed and ran to hide behind his mother. We all laughed. All I could do was a greeting. I couldn't even ask, "How are you?"

That afternoon six of them were at the meeting. I preached on John 10, the Good Shepherd: how He left heaven for us was crucified and resurrected for us, and now He is the only Way, only Truth and only Life. (They like to add Him to all their other gods). Dyva translated.

After the service Diane and I prayed for people. One of the ladies I prayed with kept collapsing at my feet, pathetic, and hopeless. Dyva said, "She is full of demons."

Then evangelist John took her by the hair, looked in her eyes and very loudly said, "Satan, you get out of her, along with all your demons in Jesus Name!"

Dyva said to me, "We will fast and pray for her until she is free. We did this for our neighbor lady who had demons, and she is free and a good Christian now. We also did this for a man who was a magician and cast spells on people. He lost his power, but has not come to Christ yet."

Some of the ladies told me that my purple flowered sari made me look like an Indian. I was taking this as a compliment when they said, 'but really you need to put a half cup of coconut oil in your hair, part it in the middle, slick it back, and then instead of Nike's put on sandals and you will really be Indian! I never made the grade.

Kodali baptism message changes me.

A Christian lady in Kodali invited us to a feast in remembrance of her murdered husband. This good man cared about justice for the poor. The communists hated him because he would not cooperate with them. So a year ago they jumped him from a side street and with a long sword cut off his head.

A hundred and twenty people were crowded on her porch sitting tightly together. An evangelist spoke twenty minutes, we did some singing and then "sister Pearl will give a message of God's Good News". I spoke on: By Adam came death, but resurrection through Jesus. I dare not speak less than an hour. Dyva gave enthusiastic interpretation.

It was dark by time we got home. We had rice then collapsed on our cots for half an hour; then it was prayer time in church. We sang awhile and Dyva said, "Sister Pearl, speak to us about prayer."

So I talked about Jesus interceding for us, the Holy Spirit praying for us with yearnings and groanings that cannot be uttered. Dyva could hardly interpret he was so tired. After an hour we all went to bed. But in the middle of the night I heard people praying. All the children slept on the church floor, but the praying however loud it may get with the drums didn't wake them.

In the morning I asked Dyva about the praying in the night. He said, "We prayed between twelve and three. You must stay healthy so God can use you here, therefore we pray!" And I had peeked up at the moon, turned, and went back to sleep!

Hyderbad provides fruit trees.

Diane and I decided that it would be well for Dyva to have fruit trees on his church property to enhance their dietary needs. He said,

"We have to go to Hyderbad to get them." The four of us boarded a bus to Hyderbad. Ahh, the striking pictures along the way! The rice fields were lime green, and the ladies weeding in them were clothed in red, orange, green, and blue colored saris. I took picture after picture including the buffalo munching grass along the "freeway". However, the juggling and bouncing of the bus made most of them blurred: Not to mention the bus slamming on brakes to accommodate a cud chewing cow taking a siesta in the middle of the road.

We were enjoying the beauty when suddenly we saw the "pipe city" along the road. Hundreds of sewer pipes about 5 feet in diameter, and 15 feet long were "home" to thousands of poor people. Huts made of rags and other refuse flank them. Diane said, "Can you imagine what the temperature is in those pipes in the middle of the day?"

"I can't. Right now it's 107 here." Oh Lord, You said we'd always have the poor with us. I ache for them. I wish so I could do more. But I think You want me to concentrate on Dyva's needs. Then he will be able to give them the greatest riches of all…You.

We arrived at the research center and the gatekeeper said, "Its lunch time, you cannot go in." We waited an hour in the blazing sun, while Dyva and Diane reasoned with the man to let us in. He relented after an hour.

The man greeting us inside knew English fluently. He was absorbed in his research for hybrids, use of fertilizers, rotation of crops, and prevention of soil erosion. He said, "Here we only deal in semi-arid crops like millet, grey ground peas, and maize.

He brought us to the "canteen" where I bought rice, lamb chops, chicken curry, drinks and chapattis for seven people for $8.00! Then he said, "The research station for fruit trees is twenty miles down the road."

Dyva's cousin, James and wife Silome, had met us at the bus stop where we hired a taxi. Now, eight of us piled into the compact car meant for four. Diane asked, "Is there a nursery around closer where we can buy trees?"

Our guide said, "Not good. Why spend seven years raising a mango and it doesn't bear well?"

Please God let us buy trees at the research center for Dyva's orphans. We arrived. The gatekeeper scowled and would not let us in. I said, "We are from America and we have come to see this place and buy some trees."

A determined look crossed his face, "No sale! Hot season now."

Lord, open these gates to us please, for the sake of your little orphans whom Jesus loves. A man from the street arrived, and invited us to come inside to wait for the Boss. Perhaps he felt pity for our beet red faces in that relentless sun. Under a fan I asked about his research. He had just gotten his doctorate on some aspect of mango leaves. As he launched into his favorite subject, he informed us that they had developed 400 varieties of mangos, and then the headman arrived.

Please Jesus, don't let our trip be in vain! I asked the man, "How in the world did you manage to develop four hundred varieties of mangoes alone?"

He explained, "We grow seedlings about two feet tall. Then take a shoot from a hybrid tree. These shoots are sent to us from all around the world. We splice it into the side of the natural shoot, cutting off the top of the seedling. After two months the cut off shoot sends out new leaves of the same quality as the grafted shoot from the main stalk. So then we don't need the grafted shoot anymore. So we cut it off and we have a new tree!"

He was thrilled to find such an eager audience. We spent several hours listening to him. I for one was enthralled with what they were doing, and I got some hope that his research might someday help the residents of Pipe City. Dear Jesus, bless this man's work so more people can be fed.

I said, "We would like to buy trees for Dyva's orphans and widows. He has a well that does not run dry and his orphans can water the trees as often as needed."

In the end he sold us two mango trees, ten papaya, two beetlenut, ten guava, four limes, ten passion fruit, two jack trees, and five falsa plants. That was all we could carry in the trunk of that little car. The car had no springs as eight (including the driver) piled in and headed for James' home. James offered us a bed and meal. Dyva accepted.

Silome, hospitality 'par excel lance', managed a gourmet meal after nine p.m. Diane and I had all the energy sucked out of us by the sizzling sun, and just wanted to sleep in. They offered us their bed, a piece of plywood. Dyva and Sarah slept on the cement floor next to us. How many positions can one try in one night? The night was plenty long after all!

In the morning we saw the famous museum, and the artwork was so outstanding I could hardly tear my eyes away. But Dyva sat in a corner to read a book from Billy Graham. He said to me, "Museums are not evangelism!"

After that we went shopping. We even found toilet paper, believe it or not. The man had to get a stepladder to get at it—that is not even the last thing on their list of needs! Diane purchased combs, toothbrushes, tongue cleaners, soap, and bags-for-school-books, for the orphan children. Then she hired a golf cart taxi to get us to the bus station.

The golf cart was not too different from being on a roller coaster. Their short-turn-steering weaved us like a shuttle between ox cart, bicycles, trucks and pedestrians. I pulled my elbow in just in time as a truck swiped by with only an inch to spare. A pedestrians' robe slapped my knee as we whisked by. Darkness descended. Oxen, carts, pedestrians, goats, buffalo and bicycles didn't have lights. We missed them after they appeared in the very dim headlight, but it made my heart skip. I closed my eyes. Oh Lord, we need your guardian angels. We are out of control.

They put the plants on top of the bus. We got home 6:30 a.m. The morning prayers were almost over. Diane gave her gifts to the children. Her heart is so soft with love for these children! We slept most of the day. I summed up my experiences of the day this way:

RICH MAN-POOR MAN

Children encircled me, little brown hands reached up, open palms begged. I've filled the hands with bananas, but empty hands endlessly replace them. Here I was in love with a crowd of little children I've never met before at an intersection in Hyderbad, capital of Andhra Pradesh, India. Dancing eyes pleaded, hopeful, and expectant. But my supply of bananas was gone. My hands, their temporary pot of gold, emptied.

I wished I could gather all these thin brown bodies in my arms, on my lap, against my aching heart, while their hearts could still dream. But then what? God, there are so many of them. Where will YOU start facing their great need Jesus?

I felt a helpless, tearing feeling in my heart. *I must not let them get to me. I must look past these earnest brown eyes…open hands so warm touching mine.* But still I heard the little voices, "Ama, ama — Mama food, food."

So I looked away — and saw a man sit without legs, on a board with casters. He held his palms up to a man walking by in a crisp white suit. The rich suit saw nothing. He avoided looking. The burning sun bounced light rays off the diamonds on each hand. His chauffeur opened the door to his air-conditioned limousine. He shut the door, stared ahead, closed himself off from the too obvious needs.

The ragged beggar propelled his board to me, hands 'walking' the dirty street. To wash them with soap and water was an unthinkable luxury for him. So he held up his soiled, calloused hands begging for one more day of life. I gave him my last coin, and turned away so he couldn't see my eyes. Is this living?

My beggar will go home tonight to the sewer pipe houses or rag huts where the poor crowd together, bound by futility: his community marked by the smell of sewage, sweat and dust. The white suit will have the gate to his palatial house opened by a servant, will stroll through his rose garden and loll in cool, wine sipping self-sufficiency. The high fence around his house protecting him against contamination of fellow humans. *God, you tell us to feed the hungry, clothe the naked, heal the sick, preach the Good News to the poor. I don't know where to start. My heart aches for these dear people, but a part despises this rich white suit. He was born here. Can't he care?*

And one day my beggar will expire under the weight of despair and hunger. One day too, the rich man's blood vessels will explode or his heart suffocate under the excessive load of too much of everything. Both will die. What then?

A blind beggar touched my arm, "Ama, ama."

I had nothing left! I turned, and ran down the street, the one the limousine just took. I've had enough of open hands I can't fill. Alas, I cannot escape running into intersections with the same painful choices everywhere! Six old leprous women approached me, holding the wire handles of tin cups on arm stumps. I dare not look again. They don't even have hands to beg. If I let myself feel with them, my heart might break. So I pray, *Lord, if You can teach me how to be helpful to these precious women, I'll be glad to obey you.*

Taxi! Taxi! Let me escape. Forget. I want to smell the roses: exchange my blue, wet, sweat clinging sari for a clean one. But it would get stained with blood from my heart, for it has been pierced by their need. I wonder if the white suit wears a coconut shell around his heart to protect it from being stabbed again and again.

Lord Jesus, You didn't run away ... You did something. Oh, You didn't change the Roman rule, nor develop a better economy. You met individual needs: the blind, the leper, the demoniac, one by one. You had godly power to do more, You created universes! But You left us an example. Oh yes, You took one boy's lunch and fed 5,000.

But this is me, Lord, critical me, and now I look through a taxi window so I don't touch the warm little hands, the dirty hands, and the leprous stubs. I want to escape the wretched pain in my heart. But your heart must pain, too, Lord. What can we do?

Back at evangelist Dyva's house I scrubbed my shoes in Clorox, and tried to forget the city. I discovered Dyva has the tormenting pain in his heart too. His heart pains for the needy in his village, especially little children and widows. For years he has heard Christ's words "inasmuch as ye have done it unto one of the least of these, you have done it unto Me." Dyva still tries, but he too runs out of rice and bananas.

Lord, how can we start, here, with this food need? Land! Of course land here grows three crops every year. I go to Dyva and ask him, "If we could get more coconut, mango and banana trees to plant on your property, and if we could buy some land to raise rice and split peas, would you be able to raise enough crops to feed your orphans and widows?

With tears he says, "Yes".

I asked, "Do you have men in your church who could farm it? Who know how to get the best out of the land?

"Yes, we have such men."

I said, "When you can feed more people, do you feel a desire to expand your ministry to widows and orphans by having a building separate from the church to house them?"

He said, "That is my dream. Only God can make it possible." He called Sarah, and we went to the roof of his house to pray. We decided to pray for two acres of land. Nice land lies across the canal from his place. I prayed for that. But Dyva said, "Communists own that, they will not sell."

I said, "Then I will at least pray that that tower with hammer and sickle on it will fall over in the wind. It's a disgrace to God's good earth."

Dyva said, "Hindu's also will not sell to a Christian. We must pray for a Hindu who will buy for us." We got on our knees and poured our hearts out to God.

God did open the possibility through a Christian man who would sell two acres, but it costs $6,000. 1 had only $10 left, but it was enough to make out the agreement papers. Lord Jesus it is my lunch. Please take it and feed your 5,000.

When I went back to America, I was asked to speak at different churches to raise the $6,000.00. Dyva wrote that the deal fell through because the man's sons would not let him sell their inheritance. So we still needed a Hindu man to make a transaction for Dyva. God, like usual was working out these details way ahead of our asking. *He not only sees but **God starts answering before we get around to asking Him.***

On the first meeting at Dyva's church where I spoke, a lady came up afterward and asked us to come to her home and pray for her sick buffalo calf. Dyva explained that a buffalo calf was their only bank account. So we followed her in the twilight to her calf. Dyva anointed it with oil; I put my hands around its belly and prayed, "God please heal this little calf so this husband who is Hindu will know that You are the only God that is alive and powerful." No sooner had I taken my hands off the calf then it lifted its tail and pooped out a pile of round worms of some kind. The man danced with joy and shouted, "It's a miracle. It's a miracle."

Now when he heard about Dyva's desire to buy land, this Hindu men offered his services, and guess what land he bought? Yes, right across the canal with the communist tower! It cost $6,500.00. The wind didn't blow it down. Christians demolished it.

Also, I helped lay the cornerstone for the new widow and orphans building. I cautioned Dyva. I said, "I am not a fund raiser, and I do not have a clue how God could provide money for this building through my efforts. However, I do believe God wants your orphans and widows to have a roof over their heads, so your church is always free for meetings and prayer."

Jelle Mensonides in Tacoma, Washington sold a lot he had, and gave me the check saying, "This is for Dyva's orphans and widows home. I hope it is enough." I sent it with the suggestion that they make it two stories so the children could sleep on the roof, and that they put plenty of rebar in the cement so that it could withstand a hundred and twenty-five mile an hour hurricane wind. They did, and the next year two hundred poor people safely huddled in it during a hurricane while all their houses blew away.

Kodali baptism changes me.

Dyva said, "Tomorrow you give strong message on 'baptism'. Here people don't want to offend their Hindu relatives so they postpone baptism and remain secret believers. Secret believers are not strong for Jesus. You give powerful message."

In studying the verses on baptism it struck me that Jesus said, "make disciples of all nations baptizing them in the name of the Father and the Son and the Holy Spirit." Matthew 28:19. And in Mark 16:16 Jesus says, "He who believes and is baptized will be saved."

And Peter in his sermon on the day of Pentecost said, "Repent, and let every one of you be baptized in the name of Jesus Christ for the remission of sins, and you will receive the gift of the Holy Spirit." Acts 2:38 Every Christian desperately needs the power of the Holy Spirit to live a Christian life.

Many here could lose their lives if they are baptized because their Hindu relatives will starve them or make sure they accidentally die. But without baptism and the power of the Holy Spirit how can they live an obedient Christian life? Lord, it seems like you don't want your followers to be afraid. You want them full of power, and full of faith that You are in every circumstance with them. *Lord, baptism and preaching don't cost me my life because I'm going back to free America. You know my parents baptized me as a baby, but now I want to identify with the Indian believers and be baptized as a public sign that I believe.*

I said to Dyva, "In my message I will invite believers to obey Jesus and be baptized. I also wish to be baptized, and will invite them to join me. Where will you baptize, and what day?"

He said, "How can it be that you are not baptized?"

"I was baptized as a baby, but I have long felt that Jesus wanted me to be baptized by immersion as a testimony to my faith in Him. Gossip travels fast here. I don't want to be identified with Indira Ghandi, Mrs. Thatcher, or an American Tourist. I want to be known as a Jesus Christ believer like you. God said, "Blessed are they that do My commandments. They shall have a right to the tree of life"."

"That is very good", he said. "We will do it in the Krishna River on Wednesday."

During the speech I said, "Hindus wear a red dot on their foreheads telling the world they worship snakes, birds, frogs, graven images, and idols of manifold types. Many Hindus want to embrace Jesus in addition for extra safety.

But there is only one way to the God who created heaven and earth, and that is through Jesus buying us back by His death on the cross. Baptism symbolizes the removal of the red dot, cleanses from all sin, nothing but the blood of Jesus' is needed. And baptism tells the world that you have resurrection life in your living Lord Jesus who is coming again to take you up into His mansions prepared for you. Will you obey Jesus, be baptized and tell the world that you serve a living, loving God?"

A young lady came up for prayer…no red dot. I prayed in English and she suddenly sobbed uncontrollably. I held her close praying in tongues. When she grew quiet I kissed her forehead. She smiled.

Dyva came over and said, "She comes to the meetings, but her husband persecutes her terribly. He is trying to force her away from Jesus. She has much trouble." *And I am asking her to obey Jesus and openly be baptized! Her heart wants to. But what will it cost her? Certainly more trouble and probably her very life!*

On that Wednesday he said, "There is another woman who wants to be baptized with you. She will meet us there."

As we walked the two miles we passed a village completely surrounded by cement walls. I felt a chill and asked "Why these walls?"

He said, "It is a Communist village. Often they throw stones at me when I walk by. They hate me. They will be curious about you and Diane. It is good they can see you baptized."

A couple dozen Christians joined us after that village and started singing hymns as we walked along. Then I stood at the edge of the river with my Indian 'sister' who would be baptized with me. About thirty Communists sat on the rivers edge a block away to watch. Dyva and a few elders waded into the river, and a vigorous discussion took place. Then Dyva came to get us.

I asked, "What was the discussion about?"

He looked sheepish, "Some thought we should go deeper into the river since you are so tall. But I don't know how to swim."

I laughed, "I know how to bend my knees. We'll manage just fine."

When the water was waist high for him and thigh high for me he said, "Do you believe Jesus Christ paid for your sins and has given you eternal life?"

I said, "I do with all my heart believe I'm forgiven and have eternal life."

Dyva ask, "Will you obey Jesus Christ no matter what the cost?"

I answered, "Yes. God helping me I will obey no matter what the cost."

Dyva inquired, "Even if it costs you every family relationship, and your job, will you obey Jesus Christ?"

"Yes, I will obey Jesus even if it cost me my family and job, and I have nothing to eat."

Then Dyva raised this question, "Will you obey Jesus even if it costs you your life?"

"Yes, even if it cost me my very life, I will confess Jesus as my Lord."

As I went under the water he said, "I baptize you in the name of the Father, and the Son and the Holy Spirit. Amen."

I came out of the water feeling free, eternally washed, and full of joy, raised my hands and shouted, "Hallelujah".

He asked my Indian 'sister' the same questions and baptized her. Then he said, "Sister Pearl, she wants you to give her a Christian name."

So I said, "Jesu Ellen" which means she is 'Jesus' light'." We walked out of the water with our arms around each other. The Christians on shore said, "Now you are really one of us. You are now a member of Jesus Christ's Church in India." I may struggle over words, but I am certainly one in heart with them. And it is for eternity.

Jesu Ellen who died within the year of her bapism.

The next Wednesday we went to a small Hindu village three kilometers away. One old skinny Christian lady met us saying, "When I heard you were coming I left my relatives and hurried home. When you didn't come Monday I thought I would not see you." She laid out mats on the dusty earth. The village was poor, the courtyard not swept, chicken and buffalo smells dominated, the huts were run down with chunks falling off the sides. Little boys and girls sat on the dusty ground with bare bottoms. Dyva's two brothers and son began beating the drums and we sang.

The old grey haired lady looked to the fields where everybody else was working late because it had rained. Soon they came straggling in, but most stood outside the courtyard. So I began to speak. I shared that as a young girl milking cows, working in the fields, and doing dishes I could not believe God really loved such an insignificant little child. Why would the Creator of heaven and earth care about me? I hoped He cared. All people deep inside long to walk and talk with God. But when they don't know Him or how He sent His Son they try to find Him their own way by worshipping the sun, moon, stars, snakes, birds….all things the Creator Himself made. They miss knowing His love.

This made God very sad because He wanted to walk and talk with His people again. So He asked His Son if He would become man, go to earth, and pay for all their sins so God could have His people close to Him again. This is how much God loves you. Today He has sent me to tell you He loves you and wants to walk and talk with you.

So you pray like I did, ask forgiveness, invite Jesus into your life and tell God you want to walk and talk with Him. Also, He said, "I am coming again with angels blowing trumpets, and every eye shall see Me," you in India and I in America. I tell my grandchildren, "I don't know when He's coming, but if I die first, know this: I'll rise from the grave with a new body first and be caught up in the air. Then I'll wave and call down to you; "Look! This is the day we talked about. Come now, let's go into His glory."

I'm telling you this because I want to see each one of you here in India caught up with me into His presence. You can read all about it in this His Bible, which I now give to you. Then I gave all the children a Gospel, and to the four women in the yard a New Testament. I loaded up my arms and went outside the yard and gave a New Testament to a blue sari-ed woman carrying her scythe, a purple sari-ed wrinkled and perspiring woman with a child on her hip, a woman with a big basket on her head filled with black peas and her lunch bucket, a man with a load of hay on his head, and another skinny, older man staring at me,(I smiled) and he took the book hesitantly.

I felt exhilarated at putting the powerful Word of God in the hands of twenty-five adult Hindus and gospels into the hands of all their children. Then I prayed with the little old skinny Christian lady and she wept with joy. I also prayed with the four Christian women in the yard, who were encouraged. They didn't understand English, but they knew my Savior.

Dyva said, "They suffer much persecution in this village because of their faith in Jesus."

One is too many sometimes.

We were nearly home when we stopped at a very poor hut to greet a Christian family there. They had three little girls, seven, and five and one year old. The mother pushed her five year old toward me pleading earnestly. The little girl's brown eyes were wide with fear and she hung back against her mother's body. Dyva was embarrassed but interpreted, "They are very poor and cannot afford to feed three children. She wants to give you this child."

Diane was horrified and said, "We will pray that there is some way God can help you keep your child."

The woman pleaded even more earnestly and Dyva said, "She says that maybe you don't want this child because she has scares on her arms from being burned. She would then be willing to give you her oldest, she is beautiful."

Oh my God, what would I do in her place? And what would I do with a terrified child who cannot understand a word of my good intentions?

When I went to the city I inquired of the officials about adoption. The upshot was that it was a long process. But then I learned that if I had a thousand American dollars it could be arranged before I left! I had only ten dollars left.

All too soon I was walking between those "guardian angels with their rifles" and boarding a plane for New Delhi. That airport was big, dirty and understaffed. I waited in line two hours to have my passport stamped, then in another line for an hour and a half to have my body almost naked patted down, and my stuff dumped out of the suitcase and left for me to re-pack. Finally I was in the line for two hours to present my ticket, then I was steered into another line for two hours for a Boarding pass, and exhausted I stood another hour to get into the waiting room for our flight. I looked with envy at the guys lying on the dirty floor getting a little rest. How I wished I could join them. Never have I been so tired.

A man moved over so I could sit in the waiting room. A lady with a shawl broke her sandwich in half and gave it to me. I said, "Thank you and Wandanamalu" but she just smiled. The man sitting next to me poured half his coke in a paper cup and gave it to me. I tried to show appreciation, but it was awkwardly done.

In Holland my sister in law didn't like my sari, and took me shopping. I found myself walking down the street looking over my shoulder to see if there were little begger-children following us. Soon she had me properly clothed.

Our friends, Pier and Janke came to visit and gave me some money to get home. Very soon I was flying over the arctic to my dear hubby.

We settled down in our home in Bellevue, and in the following chapter I picked out a few snippets from our lives while living there. God never stopped being busy making Himself real to me always being one step ahead.

CHAPTER TEN

SNIPPETS ABOUT GOD'S RELIABILITY

❦

Near death on the Suattle river has one benefit.

Cold, exhilarating Suattle river water splashed over our warm bodies in the commercial rubber raft. Rits, Cal and I in front heard Julie whoop, "Aaaah,", as a wave of icy water slopped into her lap. This River Rafting Company took all it's leading rafters, including our Karen and her boyfriend Bruce, on an initial run of the Suattle. We just went along for the ride on this fourth of July.

Ross, our guide taught us to obey commands. He yelled, "Back paddle. Hard. Stop!" We obeyed.

Then we heard Karen on the other side hoot from her boat, "ohhh, ohhh", as the wave splashed over into her lap.

I thought: *Ross knows just how to get everyone a little wet and give us all a good time white water river rafting. The Cascade mountains and the river moss make magnificent scenery here near Darrington, Washington. Oh, there's a nice curl coming up straight ahead.*

"Paddle ahead", demanded Ross, "stop paddling". He continued, "I said 'please' before we got on the raft and that holds for all day." We laughed, but mostly in anticipation of the bigger waves coming up.

I heard Karen's voice call, "Hang on Mom". I grabbed a strap and leaned way back so if anything happened I'd fall into the middle of the raft.

Splash! Splash! Plop! Plop! I was over my head in water. I held the camera high in one hand. Rits gasped for breath on my left. Calvin, bobbing in his life jacket on my right, yelled, "Keep your feet forward, Mom". *How did we get here?* I reached out to Rits, and we grabbed hands. This was for real. We were at the mercy of churning white water.

Suddenly a monstrous white curl swept over our heads. My head and shoulders were pounded backward deep into the water. I lost sight of Rits. A rock hit our hands and ripped them apart.

I struggled to find top and breathe. Just then my head broke water and I gasped for air getting three-fourths air and one-fourth water. I swallowed the water as the next wave sucked me under.

Again and again I gasped for breath to get half water and half air because there wasn't time to grab a whole breath between the unruly waves. Seeing a big rock I grabbed for it. But the water was playing with me, letting hope rise and then whisking me off under the next fierce curl.

Calvin appeared to my right shouting, "Hang in there Mom, you're in good position". The next wave swallowed us together.

Head out, I used up my gasp to bellow, "I'm alright. We'll make it". Under again. There was only room for five thoughts in my head. *Where's Rits? Can he make it? Keep your feet forward. Ride it out. It will end soon.* I didn't know this white water was a half-mile long!

My seat hit a rock hard. Adrenalin pumped at the thought of shallow water, and I tried to grip my feet on ground, but the relentless water pitched me on my face and roughly threw me under another wave.

"Feet up, downstream", I command myself, "ride it out". I felt Calvin grab my foot, and saw his face full of concern. I knew he would do anything for me if he could. But it was not his choice, for the river ripped us apart with rock and rapids. I lost sight of him.

Now thoughts froze: *feet downstream—.head up—breath.* I'm in survival mode—no sense of cold or fear.

I heard a voice behind me, " Over here", and I reached toward the voice behind me. Kimberly, guide from another raft, grabbed me against her boat. But my legs were swept under the raft and I couldn't help Kim get me into it. She turned me on my back and yelled, "Kick your feet out." My legs refused to obey me! I was angry at my legs.

I heard her scream to her crew, "Back paddle, hard, harder!" I saw a partly submerged tree rush at us. *If only I could swing my legs over it.* They wouldn't budge. My miserable body was betraying me when I most needed it. The log smacked me in the stomach, doubled me over it, and slapped me face first in the water. I felt the raft slide over my shoulders. I was too tired to pray.

When my head emerged I heard Kim yell nearby, "Keep your position and—" her voice drowned as my ears filled with white water. I was spent—exhausted—wholly used up. One thought: *keep your head up.* I was enveloped in misty whiteness. Time was no more.

Julie's voice first dimly, then strongly, penetrated the whiteness, "Mom, get the rope. Mom! Mom, grab the rope."

I saw it fly ahead of me, and the water began to pull it away. By some miracle my heel hooked it, and the current spun it in reach of my hand. I grabbed a lock hold while Julie pulled me upstream to the raft. The water cascaded over my head—*I can't make my head lift. I wonder if I'll drown before they get me to the raft,* but then Ross reached out and yanked me with a great adrenalin rush right into the raft.

Air! Free flowing air! They beached the raft and laid me on the sand. I saw hairy legs trembling next to me. It's Cal! "Mom, are you O.K?"

"Sure, Cal. Need to—catch—my breath—you?"

"I'm fine", comes through chattering teeth.

"Where's Dad?"

"He's O.K."

The people slipped out of focus. My head throbbed. Then I saw the blue and green haze turn into sky and trees. And there above me I focused on friendly faces.

"Where's my husband?"

"He's out. They got him. Don't worry."

"I don't see him. Cal, where's Dad?"

"Other side of the sand bar. He's still too tired to walk over here. He was picked up further down stream. He is all right though. I saw him."

Karen's face appeared tear streaked, and I smile relief to see her. She says, "About the time Cal and Dad were rescued I landed on some shoreline rocks. When I stood up I saw you float by, white-faced, limp, appearing unconscious. I ran down the shore screaming as loud as I could, 'Get Mom, Get Mom!' Then Julie threw you the rope. Do you hurt anywhere Mom?"

"No. I'm fine honey!"

"How about your stomach", inquired Kim, it must hurt the way you womped that log."

"Can't feel any hurt." Then I give the Suattle river some of its water back with my lunch as a bonus. I overheard plans for getting to an access road somewhere downstream. *I am certainly not going to be carried out of here. I shall walk.* I sat up, and when the spinning stopped said, "I'm ready."

We walked to the raft, but dizziness forced me to sit on a rock. *Why does my body quit on me like this?* Someone, eager to be helpful says, "A person can get dehydrated through an experience like this. Here, have a drink."

One swallow of water and my stomach said, I've had enough of THAT, and it threw out a lot more of the river — and some more — and more. My head cleared. *Now I'm finally revived.* I got in the raft and sat in the middle twisting fingers under straps. We needed to go fifteen minutes to get to the access point where a road is a quarter mile away. The wind refreshed me. Then chills shook me: teeth chattering, shivering, bone cold chills. Sally put her wool shirt on me, but the shuddering persisted. Still, the ride was a bit of a thrill, and when we got to the access point I said, "Really, we could just as well go on with the river. I'd rather not have to walk!"

But Ross shook his head. "Julie and Karen have already been dispatched through the woods to get the van." I stepped on shore. My legs folded. This was embarrassing, and disgusting.

Kim laid out some wetsuits and let me rest on them. She told me how she tried to rescue me. "Just as I was about to pull you in, the tree got you. I didn't see the tree. But after we were in the water I pulled you to one side, because the water was sucking you toward that logjam. I couldn't have reached you there."

Rits held my hand wordlessly. Cal threw a blanket on me. Then others threw their wool shirts on me, and their caring warmed me.

Cal said, "When I lost you, I concentrated on riding it out. About the same time as the boat got Dad, and Kim was trying to get you, another raft caught up with me, and snatched me into their boat."

"What were your thoughts, Cal?"

"I was so concerned about Dad and you I hardly remember anything else. When I grabbed your foot I had hoped to push you into an eddy."

I heard someone from the woods shout, "The van is coming."

Ross said, "This looks like about the easiest way to go to me; I've checked it out around here."

I got up feeling refreshed. We climbed the bank grabbing ferns and tree roots. I think: *Great, I'm recovered.* Once on top we walked about fifty feet and I reached out for Rits and Cal's arms for my knees were turning to rubber. We rested on a stump. *Stupid body. What is wrong with you? Why are you embarrassing me?*

We started walking again, but Ross and Cal each put an arm of mine around their necks and practically carried me through the thistles to the van. How helpless and tired I was. The steel floor of the van felt like soft sand. *It's so good to lie—so wonderful to breath.*

Rits sat next to me, supporting my head. He told me about his rescue. "I was further down the river having been caught in the swiftest current," he said, "At first I thought this was all a joke. Perhaps we are at the end of our trip and they are dumping us out as a final good joke to end our fun. But when I saw you holding up your camera, I knew this was no joke. I held on to the paddle, and got my knuckles rapped and torn over rocks, but I think it also helped keep me more buoyant. A raft came and pulled me in. On land I had to rest. I just couldn't walk right away. They said it was O.K. to sit a bit because you were being rescued."

We meet Laura and Lorne and our three little grandchildren at the take-out point where we had our car parked. The plan had been to have a picnic supper together. I stood to tell them all is well, then bent to kiss the little three year old who ran to me with outstretched arms for her usual hug. Her eyes turned puzzled as Cal quickly helped me to a shady spot to lie down before my body dropped me. *Odd old body!*

Karen came to sit and put my head in her lap. We wept tears of relief. On the way home in the car I thought: *I didn't even pray. And what is there about riding in a car that is so exhausting?*

Home at last, I removed my wet clothes. Too tired to shower, I crawled, sand and all, into our waterbed and relived the sensations of being jerked swiftly under the curling white waves of what I once thought was the beautiful Suattle river rapids.

I never again had a nightmare about drowning. I faced the fact that I was indeed drowning. The peace that finally overwhelmed me when I was in a white fog forever dispelled that fear.

A few days later Rits asks me, "What did you learn from this experience?

"I was choosing life, but it was beyond my strength to hold on to it. I was a helpless blob, nothing more I could do, so God did it for me through caring people. That's love from Him and them."

Why is Herman leaving us?

Herman was the oldest of my Mom's brothers who lived with us. For all practical purposes he was my oldest brother. He was a stoic, strong, decisive farmer and churchman. He argued theology with the best because he kept trying to bend the paradoxes of God's Truth to his logic. His facile mind created a donkey engine to clear land, a hay hoist to put hay high up in the barn, customized trucks, could fix most anything, and designed, doweled, glued and polished a baby crib for his grandchild.

He got cancer and Daddy asked me to go with them to visit him on the fifth floor in Swedish Hospital. Herman's eyes stare out of deep sockets, the spark is gone.

Hands once strong milking cows lie white and helpless. He says, "I gotta feed the calves." He is tied to the bed like a calf roped to its stall.

Somebody says, "No I.V.'s anymore Herman?"

He says, "No you either make it here or you don't. Nobody cares."

"What did the doctor say?" someone asks his wife.

She answers, "He said, 'No more radiation. It's useless." Tenderly she says to him, "We are moving you to a convalescent center in Monroe."

He says, "I have no say I guess, people do things and take me places without my O.K." His shoulders sag. His eyes close. My heart aches for him. Oh God the rugged Herman I knew is being demolished like a dandelion crushed under a tractor tire. This disease has swept away all his hope like flood waters snatching the farmer's barn at night and swirling it away with all his cows. He needs hope.

So, I say, "Herman, are all your sins forgiven by Jesus?"

He looks my way, eyes clearing, and says, "Yes, I know I'm forgiven."

Relieved I say, "Do you realize that Jesus is preparing a place for you in heaven right now?"

There is a glimmer of a smile on his dry lips, "Yes, He is."

"Would you like us to sing a song for you Herman?"

"Yes. Sing 'Oh God our help in Ages past'. We sang all the verses of "Oh God our help in ages past, Our hope for years to come, Our shelter from the stormy blast, And our eternal home." Herman hummed along.

We left, but my heart still ached and I couldn't sleep. *Does everybody have to die helpless like this? I don't want to die like this. It is so humiliating.* I thought *the maggots of cancer are eating his strength. This energetic man I knew is like a weak, mangled calf waiting to be thrown out.*

But then, a truth dawned. I know the truth is that God is watching, serene as a sunny day at haying time. He's watching the stakes of Herman's tent decay and collapse, His gaze remains unperturbed for He knows that His Spirit united with Herman's spirit is an indestructible kernel of vivacious life. Yes, that's it. The real Herman is strong and vital.

179

Herman's spirit crouches like a runner on tiptoe, waiting to hear the last bang of the heart so it can sprint off and race into the Beloved Jesus' arms. Cut loose to see his Savior.

Kivalina, Alaska adventures with Nance, 1978

Nancy and Cal moved to Kivalina and Cal became the new principle of the school there. They invited us to "come and see", and of course we went. From Kotzebue to Kivalina we were in a four-passenger plane, which landed on a metal grid just outside the town. Nancy and a friend were there to meet us with their snow machines. I hopped on behind Nancy and away we went! Around a corner I flew off into a snow pile. *I guess I have to clamp my knees on this iron horse.* After awhile she noticed her passenger missing, and came back to pick me up, laughing.

The next morning she suggested we go on a picnic. A picnic in minus 20 degrees! We each had a snow machine. She took off across the Bay like a bat out of a cave. I gripped the handlebars not wanting to be tossed off over the bumps, and even more important wanting to keep up with her. I said, "Jesus, I hope you enjoy going fast since You are with me everywhere I go." That clear bell like thought came back, "I love it—I created the speed of light you know!"

White, white everywhere—some shafts of ice sticking up out of the Bay-ice like sentinels. Nancy stopped by a scrub willow at the beginning of the river ice. We unpacked our coffee and cookies, sat on the icy snow and picnicked. How vast is the expanse of whiteness. I had already lost track of where the village was. Nancy said, "We'll go up the river another day when my Eskimo friend Becky can go along. She never gets lost."

The sun started its short arc over the horizon. The ice on the Bay now glittered like diamonds, the 'shafts' turned into transparent marble sculptures. We stopped and stopped to take pictures. Then the sun turned the ice crystals into shattered rainbow colors! I couldn't get enough of the wonder of snow in color. I took all kinds of pictures, until my camera froze up being too long outside my parka. Just as well, the camera couldn't capture what I experienced anyway.

A few hours later the sky was ablaze with red, orange, purple, turquoise, and everything in-between. The mountains in the far distance were royal blue, the scrub willows orange, the old gray fish racks in the village gleamed like exquisite ivory art.

My God, You are lavish with Your colors here where I thought there would only be myriad shades of white. And as if You lack time to display Your whole show during the day, You hang swaying curtains of color in front of the stars. Even the Psalmist struggles to praise You enough, and though his words help me, they are not near enough. But You see my heart, You feel the adrenalin rush. What a wonder You are!

Kotzebue, Alaska is where I get to have an adventure with grandson Shad, 1980.

Cal was made principle of Kotzebue high school, and so moved away from Kivilina. Kotzebue was noisy compared to Kivalina. Here dogs barked in small yips, and deep growls, and sled dogs howled. Planes took off with the reverberating sound of jets, and there was the high pitch of ski planes, the drone of wheel planes, and the flop-flop of a helicopter like clothes whipping on a clothesline. Noises also of Teen-agers on three wheelers; front wheel in the air, black hair flying, capturing the feeling of being "in control" and being "free".

The back up beep- beep of a truck fixing electricity was accompanying the wind whispering secrets over the tundra. The crashing of waves against barges spraying out rainbows, the whistling of wind through the TV antennas, and the high-pitched sound of the water siren going on for hours until the danger of low water pressure is over (turn it off-turn it off!) causes me to pull my stocking cap over my ears.

Nine-year-old Shad, my grandson, invited me to ride in his plastic boat on the lagoon. We left the noise behind carrying the boat. At water's edge we inflated it with a bicycle tire pump. I pulled my knees up tight to get us both in the boat. For two hours Shad chatted and rowed. He shared books he has read, thoughts he has, joys, hopes, and dreams. I was immensely privileged to participate in his life.

He wanted me to see "his lake" so we hit a soggy shore and he told me, "we need to walk a bit". No way to stand in this tiny plastic boat, so I crawled out on the soggy tundra. Shad was excited saying, "Look Beppe, a muskrat hole! Here's where lemmings live — see their nest, and here are little highways they travel."

"What do they eat Shad?"

"Oh leaves, bark, meat, berries, about anything."

Fog rolled in as we sloshed about and listened for ptarmigan and loon, but all we heard is the roar of a plane taking off. The fog lifted and we headed back to our little boat. A motorboat in the lagoon sent waves rocking us like we were in a wooden shoe. Only a wooden shoe doesn't leak. We had a leak. We got out the pump and pumped it up some more without tipping over. We made it to shore.

As we carried the boat through town, we stopped to pet some puppies; inquisitive little faces, all colors, wide eyed, playful, cuddly, short-legged little best-friends-of-man.

We stood to enjoy the colors of the sky, and Shad introduced me to his friends. He wss proud of me, and I was even prouder of him.

We passed sled dogs on short chains hooked to their crate houses; jerking their chains, growling, barking, unapproachable, some blue-eyed, some mangy, but all acted fierce.

Shad told me about trying to train Chaco, Ungak and Wolf to be his sled dogs. He got them hooked up and Chaco dragged the team off to chase a little housedog, which he killed. The drunken owner screamed, angry at Shad. Later Chaco got loose from his chain and killed six six-month-old-puppies and ate part of them. They shot Chaco. Shad gave Ungak to their neighbor. "So", Shad says, "I just have Wolf, but he is strong enough to pull two boys on a sled. He could pull you, Beppe."

Shad hooked Wolf to his sled and I got on. All went wonderfully well for two blocks. Then Wolf saw a female dog and jerked me up a snow berm and dumped me off the other side! He was strong enough all right! An old man and his toothless wife smiled us a greeting.

We passed mobile homes, log homes, old homes and Jo Max houses on legs. Most houses had moose antlers displayed or caribou antlers stashed on the roof as a status symbol of hunting prowess. We passed big metal barge containers stashed wherever there was a bit of room, helter-skelter, until a summer barge could return them to Seattle. Rusty old cars and broken down snow machines had no place to be discarded, so become antique relics in front or back yards. And then we were home in Cal and Nancy's Jo Max house.

Lord God, thank You. You sure had a great idea when you designed family so grandparents could stay young and enjoy their grandchildren.

CHAPTER 11

GOD'S FAITHFULNESS IN BIG AND LITTLE THINGS

We buy Carnation Property, purchased 1985, built on in 1986.

Northrup Way, our address in Bellevue, was getting very busy, and we discussed living further out. Cliff asked for my ideal site. I said, "Big maple trees, big cedars, a winding driveway, a view of sunrise or sunset, and a little stream." He came up with a site on Tolt Hill Road with all but the stream. When I found out what demands the EPA would put on our property if we had even a very small creek on it, I was glad we didn't. Cliff wanted the adjoining property, which had a 250-degree view, but much of the property was on a steep slope.

Cliff negotiated the deal so our middle lot behind our Northrup house was exchanged for the two and a half acre site. We were thrilled. We were such novices when we bought the Bellevue house that we didn't even know it was sub-dividable. Rits jumped through all the hoops with the city making this transaction possible.

We picnicked on our property, and hand in hand Rits and I planned where our house would best fit, and how to make a curvy driveway. One of Rits' friends drew up plans for our two-story house. After a few months I said, "We have enough money to put in a foundation. Let's do it."

We hired Dan Rush with his bulldozer to clear the site. He was an artist with his bulldozer and preserved the old cedar stumps I wanted to keep. We found Steve and friend who were in the building business and we asked if they could put in the foundation. They said, "Yes, but you need a permit first."

Armed with blueprints, proper copies, and forms I applied for a foundation permit. They made me wait while others cut in front of me and got their permits. I learned these men were known contractors. Eventually I got my permit too.

The builders then told me they needed electricity on site, on a temporary pole.

I called Puget Power to lay the line to our house, and went to the electrical supply store to buy what was needed to put up a temporary pole. They were helpful giving me a sheet of instructions on how to put it all together. But when I called the inspector he wouldn't pass my work. I was in tears because the Puget Power men needed that O.K. to hook up the electric. Rits comforted me saying, "The power people will know what to do. We'll ask."

The Power man he asked said, "I know that inspector. Get some petroleum salve. We'll stuff every electrical nut with it. He'll pass it. This man loves petroleum salve! When he sees it he passes the pole." He even called him to come back, and the inspector quickly passed it. This job isn't so bad after all.

We planned to build as we got funds, but I found the County had a rule: once started the building had to be completed in a year. So I needed framing permit, electrical permit, plumbing permit, and on and on—seems the County wants to make money!

Our builders were also framers so they kept working.

I hauled our little fourteen-foot trailer up there so I could make coffee and when an inspector was coming early I stayed overnight. Rits was asked to be interim pastor for the Bellevue Christian Reformed Church and was too busy to concern himself about building. This was O.K. by me. I could just flounder along in my own way.

We squeeze in counseling.

A couple we knew from another state was in Seattle. They called and asked if they could come for counseling. I gave them directions to our trailer on site. We squeezed around the little table. They viewed their diverse ways of looking at the same situation as bull-headedness on the part of their partner. When that happened, they resurrected all the old garbage and tossed it into the argument as weight in his or her favor.

They were hopelessly stuck, living separated and then trying to live together again, over and over. Please God give me some creative way to get them unstuck and appreciating the love they obviously have for each other deep down or they wouldn't be here.

She was artistic and flighty. He was methodical, logical and full of common sense. She needed him to keep her feet on the ground, and he needed her to put spice in his life. But when I pointed that out they brought up all the times this difference was not appreciated, and therefore couldn't work. Lord, how can they leave the non-working past behind and press on to a creative future?

I handed them each a long sheet of paper and asked them to write all the old grievances and fights they could think of. I made coffee and encouraged them to let it all hang out. I was on my third cup before they finished. I had them read Matthew 18 where Peter asks Jesus, "Lord, if my brother sins against me how many times should I forgive, up to seven times?" Jesus answered in verse 22, "I tell you, not seven times, but seventy times seven." And then Jesus told them a parable in which he demonstrated that unforgiveness was no option. God demands we forgive as He forgives us.

I asked, "Do you want to forgive each other? Do you want to cut old garbage out of your life and look toward handling your godly differences in a fresh way?" They nodded.

She went first, "I forgive you, John for—and she read off her list. Then he did likewise, choking in emotion. They hugged and cried.

I asked, "What does God do with your sins after they are forgiven?"

She answered, "He throws them in the sea of forgetfulness." (Micah 7:19)

"Now", I said, "would you like to bury your lists and never dig them up again?"

Each eagerly said, "Yes".

I held out an empty coffee can in which they deposited their lists. I put the lid on and said, "Come outside." I handed her a shovel, "It needs to be two feet deep. The ground is soft." She'd never had a shovel in her hand before, so I was showing her how, when he gallantly took the shovel and dug the hole. She put the can in. I said, "Forgiveness that pleases God is to bury it forever just like He does. You now have an opportunity to make a deal with each other. If anyone brings up anything that's in that can, the other is to say, 'Are you willing to go to Carnation to dig up the coffee can'?" They laughed, and shook hands on the deal. She covered the coffee can. They did not put a gravestone on it!

Life was not suddenly 'living happily ever after', but they weathered the storms, and recently they asked Rits and me to fly to their state, visit them in their new home, and see their grandchildren.

More God Surprises.

Our friend Jake in Lynden took left over windows and doors from wholesalers and sold them out of his barn. He called, "I'm getting in a shipment of windows with the white cottage strips inside the two panes. If you are interested come tonight and pick out what you want." We hurried the one hundred and ten miles to Lynden with the blueprints in our hands. We picked out gorgeous windows, bigger and better than was on the blueprint. He shipped the next day, and we went home exhilarated.

The builders saw the new and bigger sizes on the blueprints and gasped, "If you had been a day later we could not have made these alterations." *Whew God, You were just on time with this blessing. You see everything and prepare in advance.* My, my, the windows have made our home into a country cottage!

Rits and I went to the Home Show and saw a gorgeous sunroom. Rits is a talker, and while I was coveting, he showed the man it was to his advantage to sell us two for the price of one and a third. We put one sunroom opening into our bedroom surrounding the hot tub. The other opened into our living room. Counselees loved this room as it was just like sitting in the woods. Rain and snow, moonshine and sunset added ambiance.

The drywall man painted everything off white. Our furniture was pretty eclectic, and I didn't have a color scheme in mind at all yet. Our friend Jake called, "What are you doing for carpet?"

I said, "We decided to wait until we could afford something decent. Chip board is fine for now."

He said, "I'll be in Seattle in a couple hours. My carpet man is moving his business across town, and has some carpet he'd rather sell than move. No color choice. If you meet me there we'll see if we can work out a good deal."

When we arrived he told the carpet man, "I want you to give this couple the same good deal as you would to one of my kids."

We found a warm brown to fit our living room…thirty year guarantee, topmost quality. It was all the highest end carpet. A tweed carpet fit our guest room. A soft purple fit our bedroom and hot tub room. He threw in a beige one for the other sunroom. Our study was 13 feet by 25 feet. He had a sea green piece 12 feet by 40. I said, "Wonderful. Bookshelves will cover that last foot, and that leaves plenty to carpet the stairs." The total cost was less than if we had bought cheap indoor/outdoor carpet!

We were higher than a kite. What a bonanza. Jake shook off our thanks saying, "I think God must like you." We felt liked and loved!

Rits nearly dies.

We were going to a minister's meeting in Lynden, 1987, with Rev. Herm and wife Melba, taking the scenic highway nine route. It was lovely though it rained hard all the way. I was driving as we neared Mt. Baker Highway. I hit a long puddle of water and hydroplaned into a six-foot ditch. Herm and I got out and got Melba out who was in shock hitting her forehead on the windshield and bleeding profusely. I scrambled up the ditch bank and hailed a truck driver who called 911.

I went back to get Rits out. He said, "Honey, I'm hurt bad. I can't move." I took off the seat belt and struggled back up the ditch, stopping a car saying, "Please help. My husband is hurt bad. We need an ambulance."

She said, "I'll find a neighbor and call immediately."

I slid down the bank, took a look at my husband's gray face and fear for his life grabbed my senses and shook them like a dog a rag doll. Anger replaced the helpless fear—anger that the car wouldn't brake, anger that I couldn't miss the ditch (if only I could have made it turn!), anger that I had not insisted that Melba wear a seat belt, anger that I didn't know how to help my husband. I hated seeing him scrunched up in the back seat. Anger that it was taking forever for help to come.

Herm said, "Don't move him Pearl, you could make things worse." I wanted to do something! Herm took my arm, "Don't blame yourself. You did what you could."

Melba chimed in, "I chose not to wear a seat belt. It's not your fault." But I was the driver—if only—if only—and now everything was in grinding slow motion!

Finally two cop cars came and their questions helped divert my fears. They said the ambulance was on the way. *Who was driving that thing anyway? Did they have the lights on? Why oh why was it taking so long?*

When they finally arrived they took Rits 'blood pressure, exchanged glances, quickly got him on a stretcher, and began an IV. His belly was bloated, face gray, sliding out of consciousness. I said, "Can't you hurry?" They said something about "stabilizing", but my heart was screaming, *hurry, hurry, stabilize on the way*! Ages later they turned on their lights and slowly headed for the hospital. I wanted them to lay a strip in haste. They did nothing in haste. *My husband can die while they are 'stabilizing'.*

One cop took Herm and Melba to the hospital, the other put out cones to warn traffic of danger, and we waited for the tow truck. She said to me, "Good thing you hit the ditch. A few weeks ago a man could not navigate this corner, swung to the left over there and ended up in the swamp. We couldn't get to him on time. I know your husband is hurt, but three of you are alive."

The tow truck came, and she took me to the hospital. They were wheeling Rits to surgery, but stopped long enough for me to kiss him and say, "It's going to be all right." But I knew in my gut he was very near death. A nurse came up to me and said, "We have to check you out to see if you are O.K." They found I had a broken nose, and other than a pounding heart was fine.

I went to the waiting room and sat praying for Rits and the doctors. Eventually I left the outcome in God's hands, but this did not diminish my anxiety. About two hours went by and in walked our son Calvin. I burst into tears. We sat and comforted each other until the doctor came in from surgery.

He said, "Your husband is on his way to intensive care. His abdominal artery was severed by the seat belt. When we opened his abdomen blood flew everywhere. I grabbed the artery to keep blood in his heart. My assistant stitched up the artery. He is getting blood transfusions. We expect him to recover. You can see him in an hour."

Calvin toppled backward in a dead faint like a big chain-sawed tree. It took him twenty minutes to recover, and then we went to get something to eat.

As we entered intensive care Rits opened his eyes, winked and then was off under morphine. Cal stayed someplace and the assistant surgeon, a friend of Rits', took me home with him. In the morning I looked in the mirror and saw two black eyes and a swollen nose that was also black and blue. I didn't look again for three days, and then it had all turned yellow.

After five days the doctor took Rits home with him and we stayed another three days so he could gain strength to make the hundred-mile trip home. I was concerned because after sitting up only a very little while Rits was exhausted. The doctor said, "It will take three months for him to recover." After three months the doctor said, "You know, it really takes six months before he is back to normal!" Whatever it takes, he's alive and I'm mighty glad.

Daddy goes to heaven.

Very early on April 1, 1988 we got a telephone call. My Mom said, "I think Daddy has died."

I said, "We'll be right there." We drove as fast as we dared, and arrived after the volunteer fire department did. Daddy was lying in bed just like he was sleeping. I took his cold hand and kissed his cold face. One of the firemen said, "He probably died after one a.m."

Mom said she got up to start breakfast, and then thought it strange that he wasn't up first as he usually was. So she went to wake him, and as she entered the bedroom she knew he was gone. Relatives and friends arrived and I wept with all of them. Rits consoled Mom. One little grandchild said, "Who is going to make sandwiches on Sunday after church if Pake (grandpa) is not here?" All of us standing in the kitchen wept again at our loss.

I thought I had gotten hold of my emotions when farmer Jake walked in. He had come straight from his barn and smelled of milk, disinfectant, and manure. He put his arm on my shoulder and said how sorry he was for us. Suddenly, my mind took me back to Daddy comforting me in the barn with that same smell. I would never hear Daddy's comforting words again! I sobbed uncontrollably. And Jake held me as long as I needed to be held.

When they took Daddy's body there was a terrible finality.

I concentrated on where he really was. He was in heaven where Jesus said he had prepared a place for him. I imagined him seeing his son Floyd, baby daughter, Ma, his brother John, and a myriad of friends who had gone on before causing him to comment to Rits and me, "I have to keep on making younger friends because my age mates have all died." He and his brother John always loved fishing together. I wondered if they would have to wait for a new earth, or would that be part of the great place Jesus had prepared, promising that it would be beyond our wildest imaginations?

Did Jesus Himself meet him when he entered that other dimension? Daddy told us that Christmas and Easter meant more to him every year. And when he saw those nail scarred hands and feet I know his heart must almost burst with thanksgiving and praise.

He loved the smell of lilacs, his favorite, and I imagined him putting his nose up to flowers surprised with new and wonderful fragrances. Hopping in the car with Mom for a trip to see new wonders was always a highlight to them. Was he now exploring even greater vistas than the Grand Canyon, Alaska, Mt. Rainier, and the wide prairies? He could never carry a tune down here. Was he shocked to hear his voice harmonize with the angel choruses?

I was not sad that he was in an indescribably wonderful place. I was selfishly sad for me. I could not hug him, I could not serve him coffee, and I could not roast a marshmallow for him. I could not go to Ernst hardware with him. I could not show him my garden. I could not tell him all the things that made me happy.

Grief is not quickly assuaged. At a program I saw a man sitting a few rows ahead and to my right. He had a baldhead with a fringe of gray hair around it. My heart stopped, I half rose, so sure it was Daddy. Of course it wasn't, but I was graphically reminded of my loss again. But it was his gain.

Mom was always first to cope when floods, fires, sickness, and accidents came to the farm. She turned into an efficiency machine to which all of us turned for advice and direction. She admirably coped with the changes a spousal death brings including a move to Monroe to a rented house my sister owned. After two years, she admitted to me, "I miss Daddy now more than ever. It is so lonely."

CHAPTER 12

GOD INITIATTES ACRES OF DIAMONDS

Acres Of Diamonds is conceived 1973, Carnation.

On my way down Tolt Hill Road to get groceries near midnight, I was struck with a memory. When I was in High School in Tolt (now Carnation) I would walk to town at noon hour. The sight of children without shoes on a frosty day caused me to pray: "God if ever you want me to do something about the plight of these children, tell me and I will do it." I gave them what I had, a candy bar each noon. That was fifty years ago! The thought came: *There are even more children now without fathers and in need. You can do something about it.* But God we are retired now, and I wouldn't have a clue even how to start.

So I looked around for someone with organizational talent who could inspire us to start a home for neglected children. In the paper I read about such a home in Sultan. The first article talked about the authorities railing on the home for requiring residents to remove horse manure from the barn before they could ride the horses. Don't these city slickers know that removing manure is part of running a farm?

Then there was an article about bringing the children to church, and the van was lacking one seat belt. Another article followed claiming the well was too close to the barn though they admitted that testing the well proved the water was good. It soon became obvious they were making excuses for shutting the place down, and eventually they succeeded. I wonder, *what is the real truth about this Christian ranch?*

We went to visit Cal and Nance in Tucson, Arizona. There we met a couple that wanted to start a home for children on their property. We helped them clean up this property, and then together we went to visit Sunshine Ranch for children near Phoenix. The manager was delighted to hear that we wanted to start a ranch too. He gave us a book on how the first couple began this vision. When I asked about the constitution and rules for running it, he gave me copies of all. Then he prayed that our venture would be successful.

Cal and Nance's friends never got the project underway. I read all the material and thought*: it is possible to get a non-profit status; we could use mostly their constitution and rules and start a home.* I needed somebody who had organizational skills. I always scored zero on tests in this area and I didn't like doing it. I was still unaware that God prized obedience above all. I thought He needed <u>some</u> skill, and I had none.

We search for direction.

We heard about a man starting a Christian ministry to men coming out of prison. We asked him to come over and share his vision with us. After a delightful time of sharing, I told him about my concern for neglected children, and what we learned at Sunshine Ranch. He said, "Don't think you can start a Christian ranch in Washington. They shut down the Sultan one with fabricated excuses when it was having many positive results. The real need here in King and Snohomish counties is shelters for women <u>with </u>their children. You can reach more children by taking their Moms too." We prayed for his ministry to men out of prison, and he prayed for us to get something started for homeless women and their children.

I asked my best friend, Joy if she would go with me to visit Women's shelters, and see how they did it. We visited from Bellingham to Tacoma. YWCA had a three-story home in Redmond. It was new, had an employment office, baby-sitting service, etc. The manager spoke vehemently to us, "Don't think you can do this. It takes lots of money, big organizations to back you, and a way to keep the funds coming in. Novices like you will never make it." *Evidently factoring in God's prodding, blessing and providence was not a part of their program.*

But others were simple homes with six to ten women with their children, or without children. A day manager and night manager pretty well ran it. However, most of them did not do any direct Christian teaching, nor help them become self-sufficient with a job, nor teach parenting skills. They also had thirty day or ninety day limitations on staying. We came away with a number of conclusions:

1. Most women can't change from homeless to self-sufficiency in ninety days. We need to offer them up to a two-year stay since it takes eighteen months plus to change habit patterns.
2. Everybody who comes in is entitled to know how to access Jesus as her Savior. Mandatory Bible studies each week should be part of the program. How else can they learn moral standards?
3. We should teach the 14-Steps, which is AA plus Jesus and His Spirit. Also AA and Narcotics Anonymous must be made available for social support to help stop substance abuse. Urine-analysis needs to be done sporadically because I'm too naïve to tell if they are using or not.
4. Budgeting must be a mandatory part as many have credit card debt, or outstanding tickets. It would also help them save for first and last months rent when leaving.
5. Parenting classes are obviously needed as most of these women were not properly parented and have no clue how to parent, or set proper boundaries.
6. Help them get their GED or a job.
7. Provide counseling.

Well, that's a start for goals. We described ourselves as 'A Christ-centered Home Facilitating Women with their Children toward Self-sufficiency.' We needed a Board to apply for a non-profit status. At least I knew how to do that. Joy (my friend) said she would be Vice President, Connie, who had just returned from teaching English in Taiwan for ten years said she would be secretary-treasurer. We couldn't find a president. I was still praying desperately for an organizer. By default I was "it" until we could find a proper replacement. Lord, I'll do this to get the non-profit status, but You have not gifted me to be an organizer. Please, please send somebody to do this leading job.

501C3 and then we were renting.

I n 1995 we were informed that we had a temporary non-profit status. We must prove after a year that we had met monthly and that our goals were being accomplished. Then we could get a more permanent status. Joy said, "Oh my, we aren't ready for this!"

I said, "We are definitely not ready. I don't even know what ready would mean. However, this is not just our idea, it is God's. He said, "Inasmuch as we have done it to the least of these we have done it to Me...feed the hungry, heal the sick, take in strangers, cloth the naked." You know Matthew 25! This is God's idea and He has to make it work. For sure, I am not smart enough. I think we should look around for a house, and if God provides that, we'll know we are on the right track with Him, and that He wants us to proceed, ready or not."

Joy and I were looking at other shelters and asking how they got their houses. Simply buying one and getting others to help pay for it was the usual way. As we passed through Duvall she said, "Let's stop by this real estate office and see if Wes Childers knows of anything."

We were thinking of Carnation since we both lived there, but he said, "Nothing there. Maybe you should think Duvall; at least it has bus service to Seattle two times a day." He found nothing, but then said, "Hold on, Dave and I own a house a few blocks away. Someone is renting now, but plans to move out in a couple of months. You could rent it to start with until you get a down payment."

We found it on the Kennedy Street hillside overlooking the Snoqualmie valley. It had five bedrooms and a full daylight basement. We said to each other, "This could be a good starter." The rent was a thousand dollars a month. Joy and I spoke at churches, community centers, Republican Women's-Club and wherever we could get people excited about helping homeless women and their children. I couldn't get myself to beg for a quarter to make a personal phone call, but I could get passionate about women and children living in a car or under a big coat on the streets of Seattle.

We buttonholed relatives and friends. One of them said, "Women <u>and</u> their children! That's a witch's brew if ever I heard of one. I can just see them pulling each other's hair out over child disputes." (No help from him!)

I hustled with a volunteer to get beds, dishes, and everything needed to make a home. Every month, somehow, the thousand dollars came in, while I kept reminding myself, *God, this is your idea, You know I can't pay for it.*

Our first three residents challenge us.

Our first resident was parked in front of my Carnation church sleeping in her car. She told me she had been wandering around the country for several months in her car. She would drive a couple hundred miles, feel sleepy, and pull off the road and sleep. Then travel a couple hundred miles more until she was too sleepy to drive. She lost track of where she was going or why. She pulled up in front of the church because she was sleepy and it was a parking place.

She stayed in the house for two months, never taking her car to leave. She slept a lot and was encouraging to me when I came to teach classes and bring supplies. One day she said, "I used to be a nurse, and I've been calling around. Next week I have an interview for a job."

When she came back from her interview she said, "When they asked why I haven't been working I told them about driving about and not knowing where I was going or why. Immediately they said, "You have been carbon monoxide poisoned"."

Sure enough there was a large hole in her muffler. Her former husband put a new muffler on, and ultimately she went back to her family: husband and three children.

The second resident was pregnant and had a three-year-old. An Episcopalian church member brought her from Seattle (all the shelters were full). I fell in love with her precocious little girl. She wanted food, clothes and transportation handed to her because she was pregnant. She wouldn't even take GED courses when I had arranged for someone to come to the house to teach her! It cost me sleepless nights to consider ending her stay because her little girl didn't deserve to be on the street. Finally I told her, "You have done nothing to help yourself. You have chosen by your actions to not live here."

She was furious with me calling me many derogatory names, and refused to budge. So I looked her straight in the eye and said, "You have refused to even slowly take courses to get your high school diploma, and you yourself said, "This program is not for me if you force me to do that." I agree with you. It's not for someone who refuses to become self-sufficient. Now, if you don't go on your own, I will take you to the car."

She got her stuff from the bedroom, her little girl looking back wistfully at her crib, and got in the car. I heaved a sigh of relief. How in the world did I expect to move a 275-pound woman to my car. Glad she didn't challenge me on that. She went to a friend's house.

The third resident called from a crack house on Capital Hill, Seattle, and said, "I went to a retreat with my neighbor and got saved. I can't stay in this house full of temptations." So I went to pick her up. I'll never forget the sight of beautiful young men and women lying on the floor spaced out as if dead. The sight of their utter stillness haunts me yet.

On the way to Duvall she said, "Stop a minute. I hear my son calling me from under the truck!" I pulled over, and she checked under the truck and saw her son was not there. She pulled out a cigarette with trembling fingers.

I said, "Let's just relax here while you smoke your cigarette. Tell me about your son."

She said, "He's eight years old. I was so spaced out the Child Protective Services took him away and put him with an older man who claims he is a relative. I was soo sure he was calling me just now."

I replied, "Perhaps the residue of drugs in your system is causing you to hear his voice. What have you been using?"

"Speed, meth, cocoaine, heroin, alcohol, and whatever I could get. But I want out now. I want to get my son back."

"We'll give you the best chance we can to help you attain those goals."

The first two weeks she was so hyper with speed in her system that she had the whole house hopping in a cleaning spree. What the devil was using to destroy her, God temporarily used to get our house clean!

Later I went with her to get more of her stuff. No boys and girls were lying on the floor this time. I sat with the owner/dealer and prayed with him. He wanted the Lord, but didn't want to leave his lucrative business. As I walked through the room where those precious bodies had been, the smell in the house, and his bad decision, made me feel like crying and puking at the same time.

A drug and alcohol counselor in Duvall came to the house and counseled this third resident. Thanks to her help resident three made it to a self-sufficient life. She began working in a restaurant until she could rent her own apartment, she got her nine-year-old son back from foster care, and found good friends and support in a church.

I was at the Acres of Diamonds house every day teaching and counseling. As residents increased I tried hard to get volunteers to stay the night in case of an emergency. Joy helped out. Rits and I did an overnighter often. Steady volunteers could not be found.

We increased the Board, and got liability insurance. Some building volunteers offered to make bedrooms in the basement, but we couldn't do anything to the house until we bought it.

Buying a House for AOD.

Rits had to preach in Enumclaw at a church that was going out of business. In fact he preached there fifty two times. I knew they would sell they would have to give the profits to another non-profit organization. So I boldly asked them if they would consider Acres of Diamonds, and explained our ministry. They asked me to send an official request, which I did with more information about buying the house and needing $25,000.00 as a down payment. Imagine my feelings of ecstasy when we got a check in the mail for $25,000.00!

Now that we had a down payment we needed a bank to give us a mortgage on the rest of the money. Each of the nine people on the Board asked their particular bank to give us a mortgage for the rest. None of the Banks would do it because we only had a nine-month record of paying rent, and no collateral beyond the house. Plus nobody on the Board was rich.

Joy and I decided to visit the new Bank in Duvall. The Banker asked, "How do you expect to pay the mortgage which will be $1,000.04 per month?"

I said, "God sees to it there is a thousand dollars a month in rent. So far He hasn't missed a month. I believe He will do the same for paying the mortgage. We need to buy this house so we can add bedrooms and make other improvements. It will be worth more next year than it is now."

Joy said, "Wouldn't you like your Bank to be part of getting homeless women and children off the streets?"

He smiled at our enthusiasm, "I want to believe with you that God will provide the money, but how can I convince the Bank Board?"

I said, "You do your best. We will pray that God incline your Board to say 'yes'."

Two weeks later he called us in. With a big smile he said, "Your prayers are answered. Except for one thing: the Board wants another $25,000.00 in cash to put aside in a special account just in case God misses a month or two."

I grabbed his hand, "It's a deal. We'll ask people to invest with promissory notes and God will provide." In three weeks time we had $30,000.00 @7.5% interest. The Bank was happy.

We had a house, and now volunteers could come and put in bedrooms and bath downstairs, and we could alter the garage and put a bedroom there too... We could then take nine women with their children. We were thrilled. After that was completed we were able to add on a large family room and extra bath, to further accommodate nine women and their children.

How true are the words of the Psalmist in Psalm 145 "The Lord upholds all those who fall and lifts up all who are bowed down." And Ps. 146 "Blessed is she whose help is the Lord God who made heaven and earth, who remains faithful forever. He upholds the cause of the oppressed and gives food to the hungry. The Lord sets prisoners free, the Lord lifts up those who are bowed down, the Lord watches over the alien and sustains the fatherless and widow, but he frustrates the ways of the wicked. Praise the Lord!"

God was doing His part, bringing in the money and changing lives. But I, I was tired, dragging my aching joints up the stairs every day: teaching, counseling, and trying to get volunteers to take over little jobs for more than a couple weeks.

We searched for a volunteer to live there, but everybody lasted only a month or two and was burned out with the intensity of life in community. We desperately needed a president who knew how to run a ministry like this. We had started a ministry that was growing and having positive results, and I didn't know how I could quit. I felt trapped.

God, You know I am totally out of my comfort zone, and I am bone tired. What can I do? I feel like laying down under a cedar tree far away and sleeping for a week at least. Help Lord! What are You expecting of me anyway?

Help!

Our daughter Laura had just finished college after a divorce, and was applying at several places for a job. I pleaded with her, "Honey, could you just help me out while you are waiting to get an interview?"

She replied, "I guess so, but doing that kind of work does not appeal to me."

After a week I said, "If you could help me two more weeks, Dad and I will pay you."

At the end of the month she had fallen in love with the little children in the house who called her 'Lawa', and found herself identifying with the women who were struggling on welfare, who suffered from issues of abandonment, and who were trying to parent while going to school or trying to get a job. She had been dealing with all these issues the last three years herself.

Plus many of them struggled with alcohol and drug addictions. In interviewing a prospective resident Laura was surprised to find herself inundated with love for her. She also was very effective in encouraging and helping these women. The Board decided to hire her half time. And God sent just that amount of money extra every month! She spent the other half-time cleaning houses and taking AOD women along to teach them how to do this. After three months I asked the Board to hire her full time, which they did. And God did His part again!

She exhibited administrative talents I never knew she had. Praise God. And I, I got to sleep in our waterbed instead of at the Acres of Diamonds Home.

We held a brainstorming session with fourteen creative people to see if we could establish a business, which could get our residents working right away. Herb farm, small cheese factory (for sale nearby), making chocolates, all of which took an initial outlay of money and someone to run it. Letter stuffing, quilting, and a garage sale, didn't take an outlay of money.

I got some gifted ladies to teach quilting, donors gave the supplies, and we had a place to sell. Only one of the women could be motivated beyond the actual teaching sessions. She sat down and made herself a vest and skirt, a crib blanket for her upcoming baby, and a quilt for herself.

So instead we got some of the women to sort out garage sale items, advertised and sold items out of a tent that was donated. We needed real supervision but couldn't find volunteers. So some of the stuff went to the women's friends, and some of the proceeds vanished. It was much easier to brainstorm ideas than materialize them! Maybe someday we'll have a bone fide business.

I was relieved of the stress of being there everyday. We now had excellent volunteers teaching Bible studies, coming to pray individually with the ladies, leading the fourteen steps, teaching budgeting, and we had a video series for the women on parenting which helped them immensely.

In spite of my laid back style of life, rheumatoid arthritis got worse and worse and the medications ceased to do any good. I couldn't even change positions in bed without terrible pain.

The rheumatologist shrugged his shoulders. *Now that's not good news.*

He said, "You have run the gamut of all the medications available for this disease. They aren't working anymore. I'll give you codeine to cope with the pain."Of course I complained to God and asked Him, *"How in the world can You turn this into good?"* I think He likes a challenge because I found out later that He was already working on it.

CHAPTER THIRTEEN

GOD'S WAYS ARE AMAZING!

We make a decision.

Finally I said to Rits, "I think we have to make some decisions. I can't take care of this place. We have to hire someone to help, or move to a smaller place. He was shocked because we had decided this ideal home was our final move. To top things off we had made a poor investment and were strapped financially. Realistically it would be hard to hire help and pay ever-increasing taxes on our house.

I asked the rheumatologist if there was anything new on the horizon so I could have some hope. He said, "I just started a new experimental program, but the only ones who qualify are people who have had the disease less than three years. You've had it eighteen years."

I questioned, "Could you ask them to make an exception?"

He sat quiet, then answered, "I guess I could ask, yes, I could at least ask. I'll do my best Pearl." If he had said a plain 'No', I could have steeled my emotions, but this tenderness made me cry! Two weeks later he called and said, "Come in, we'll get you started on the program!"

After two months of being on the shots I began to feel less pain, but dare not say anything yet. I wanted to be sure. In the meantime our son-in-law, Bruce, and our daughter, Billie, in Spokane asked us to move to their twenty-acre place and put a double wide trailer on it. Part of the reason Bruce and Billie moved to Spokane was to be near Bruce's grandparents. He wanted them close so his children could enjoy them. It turned out they were too old to want to move. He begged us to come and grandparent their twenty-three children!

We waded through the stickler weeds to the site, all the kids tagging along to not miss anything. They had named the site "dung hill" because they trained their dogs to use "dung hill" as their toilet. We could sell our Carnation house, buy a modular, dig a well and still have equity on which to live (if we don't live too long!). It seemed like God was making a way, and soon Bruce had done the legal division of land so our modular had a place. And we changed the name of the knoll to "preacher's hill". But the dogs didn't understand the change!

The shots worked marvelously well and I was full of vigor in time to move, July 4, 1998. What fun to watch Bruce and Billie's children grow. We have big windows in our modular and have watched the children learn to ride the horses, catch field mice, trap gophers, make a tree fort, make jumps for their bikes, dig a fort in the field, and jump on the trampoline. And on a summer Saturday all of them a colorful gang pulling weeds or hoeing in the garden.

How privileged we are to live right next to twenty three of our grandchildren and lavish our love and prayers on them all. I think God provided grandchildren to help us think young, and be touched by love and hugs. They will probably not understand this until they are grandparents, and then they will say, "Now I understand why Pake and Beppe sometimes got tears of joy in their eyes. As kids it just didn't make sense for them to cry when happy."

The Palmer Family

Bruce and Billie's Family

Moses is found.

Laura called me up in 2003 saying, "Mom, I'm lonesome for Moses. Vivian and I have started praying that we can find him and get in contact."

I said, "Wow! We don't even know if he is still called Moses, or if he is even alive. And if he is alive where would he be living? This is like looking for a needle in a haystack. For forty-five years we have had no contact with him. But I guess God is a mighty magnet and can find any needle in however old a haystack. I'll start praying too."

I gave her the names of the missionaries who were with us in Nigeria from 1955 to 1958. She called them all but most did not even remember the tiny boy we cuddled and loved and tried to adopt. We were left with only a prayer. You know where Moses is God, and You know who knows about him. So we trust You to find him for us. We're out of clues. We don't even know what to do next. Help in Jesus name, Amen.

A couple months went by. Laura called to say that the Spees who replaced us in Turan had called her again and said, "We just learned there is a Dr. Martin Reedyk who goes to Nigeria once a year. He lives in Alberta, Canada. If you call him he might be willing to ask around concerning Moses."

Laura called asking, "Would you like to be part of a miracle?" Then she told him about our efforts to adopt Moses forty-five years ago, and explained how much she missed her little brother. She asked, "Would you please ask people you meet if they have heard about our Moses?"

He replied, "I'll ask around and immediately email you if I get news about him. I'm going next week." We prayed. We hoped. It would indeed take a God-miracle.

After three days at Mkar hospital Dr. Reedyk remembered his promise and said to the man who cooked his food that night, "There's a forty five year old story about a baby from the Ion tribe which a young missionary family took into their home. They wanted to adopt him—"

"Oh, that's Moses!" said the cook. "He lives in Abuja, the capital, 300 some kilometers from here."

Dr. Reedyk said, "His family wants to hear from him."

The cook eagerly responded, "I will catch a lori (truck) and go to Abuja tomorrow and find him. He will want to come back and meet you."

When Moses arrived the security guard would not let him see the doctor, even though he told the guard that the doctor was expecting him. Finally Moses said in exasperation, "I want you to take this note to the doctor. If you don't I'll have you fired."

The doctor told the guard, "I've been waiting two hours to see this man. Bring him right here immediately."

That night we got an email from the doctor which read in huge letters: "Moses is found, and is a Christian. This is his email address!"

How can I praise God enough for such an astounding answer to our prayers? I caught myself singing, "What a mighty God we serve. Angels bow before Him. Heaven and earth adore Him. What a mighty God we serve!"

Joy searches for a mode of expression. My joy wanted to see him, hug him, and talk with him catching up on all we have missed for forty-five years. How? All the family wanted to see him too. So

Moses must come. Sponsoring a trip for him would give everybody a chance to meet him. We learned he had five children, and his wife had very recently died.

Six people would be too much money for plane tickets from Nigeria, so we settled on asking him to come with his twenty four year old daughter Beverley. We wanted them to come in August when we would have a family re-union.

A friend helped us pay for the tickets. Beverley and Moses finally got visas and passports, a big hassle in the inept Nigerian bureaucracy. They arrived at the SeaTac Airport where Laura picked them up. After a few days she drove them to Spokane to see us.

I heard her horn toot and ran out the front door. Moses got out of her car and ran toward me with his arms out calling, "Mama, Mama!" I ran just as fast across the lawn and my fleeting thought was: *So long ago he ran to me just like this with arms out to be picked up*. We laughed and hugged and hugged and laughed together. His laugh was just the same wholehearted laugh as when I used to kiss him on his little belly button.

Pearl greets Moses after 46 years

After the family re-union we were driving back to Spokane, and I asked Beverley, "What is your heart's desire for your future?"

Without hesitating she said, "I would like to go to college in America and become a reporter."

I looked at Moses, "Moses, do you agree with leaving her here?"

He said, "That would be a big miracle. It would be a dream that comes true."

Rits and I took them to Whitworth College in Spokane the next day. There we met Mama Beans as the students call her. I spoke at a women's retreat with her a few times so we knew each other, and she had heard how we saved Moses from starvation. I told her the rest of the story of Moses as it had unfolded these past few months, and she exclaimed, "So this is your very own Moses. The one you had to leave behind, and now look at what wonders God has done to bring him back to you!"

Beverley, Moses, and Laura.

"Yes Mama Beans, God surprised us, and his daughter Beverley wants to go to college here and become a reporter."

Mama Beans excitedly took over, and when she learned Beverley was a citizen of the United States because she was born in Kansas she exclaimed. "That cuts through a lot of red tape. What providence that she was born here."

Moses said, "I had a scholarship to Kansas University to get a Masters in Fisheries. I wanted so much to find the family that saved my life, but I did not know their name." I spent three years there, and then went back to work for the Nigerian government in the Fisheries department. My other children are Nigerian."

Within five days Mama Beans put scholarships in place, registered Beverly in appropriate classes and secured a job for her in the cafeteria. Then an unexpected opening in a dorm became available. Mama Beans said, "Beverly, God has opened every door for you here. Are you excited?"

Brown eyes big with wonder, Beverly said, "Yes indeed I am thrilled."

The college in Nigeria did not fax back her transcripts, but Moses said, "I will go there personally and push them into replying to you. That is the way in Nigeria. Everything goes very, very slowly."

As we drove home from the college Moses exclaimed, "Everything goes so fast in America. I can hardly believe my daughter has this chance of a lifetime. I am so very happy."

Once more God showed how He was watching over us as a now enlarged family.

Beverley graduated from Whitworth in May, 2006, and is now pursuing a degree in nursing.

Acres of Diamonds has a baby!

A man of God I've known for forty years said, "Pearl, if you buy a house for a Spokane Acres of Diamonds, I will give you $30,000.00 toward a down payment." I was flabbergasted and said, "We need a President, Administrator and a board first."

He said, "Let's get the house, then the rest will come." I doubt if he knew those were God's words put in his mouth.

While I prayed about it, the Duvall Acres of Diamonds made a decision to match with another $30,000.00 if we could get a "baby" started here!

I called Mama Beans since I knew she and her pastor visited the women's prison and did street ministry to the lovely women caught in prostitution. She said, "We've been praying for four years to have a home for the women who become Christians and need encouragement to launch out in new ways."

Duvall AOD offered them their constitution and By-laws, and all their teaching materials, house rules, and ways of doing in-take interviews. They were excited, and Mama Beans became president, her pastor Pat is the Administrator, and they have an accountant for treasurer. What fun they had shopping for a house.

Eventually a real-estate man actually bought them a six bedroom house with this agreement: they could pay a dollar a month rent for a year and if their ministry was up and running well, they could buy it for a dollar. He also suggested that if they ran out of space he would buy them another house.

March 19, 2007 Mama Stephanie Beans held a rousing kick-off meeting and introduced her Board members. They will open the doors to the 'Spokane Field of Diamonds, House of Blessings' in May.

After all the labor pains to get the Duvall AOD going, birthing this "baby" was rapid and painless! Now we'll watch God grow her up.

To top it all off.

Topping off my life's experiences is the privilege of praying in the Healing Rooms once a week. (healingrooms.com). I get to share with many people that God can navigate them through life just as He has our family. If they will give Him the rudder of their lives, He will get them through the densest fogs and greatest storms. When they feel like they are over their boots in manure and about to drown they need to know that Jesus cannot disown a part of Himself!

Many people are like me, jerking the sails around trying to get the ship to go where we think it should while Jesus patiently keeps the rudder steady and waits for us to wear ourselves out.

Then He whispers, My yoke is ease, <u>My</u> burdens light, why are you sweating it?

And when our most earnest prayers are not answered, He waits until we can hear His whisper, <u>My ways</u> are not your Ways, because <u>My eternal thoughts</u> are much bigger than yours.

When God took me through all the experiences you've read I believe He was preparing me for being His voice among my family and in the Healing Rooms. Now isn't that the most remarkable thing ever? He never wastes any part of our lives. He weaves all parts together, and puts <u>that</u> up as the sail. And so we sail on.

Postscript to our children, grandchildren, and great-grandchildren.

〰〰〰✕〰〰〰

Now you've read about how God steered me through my life. He kept on caring about the little farm girl He saved, and He will never stop caring about you.

I'm sure you noticed that God was always one step ahead of me preparing to give me my heart's desires, and answers to my prayers. He is one step ahead of you too. That's our heavenly Daddy.

And He is still a step ahead of Pake and me because His Son is now preparing a place for us in His mansions. And He is preparing a place for you-all in His heaven too, so we can always be together. How blessed can we get anyway? Pake and I are richer than any billionaire!

And now it's your turn to write and show your grandchildren that your Father God is faithful to a thousand generations of those that love Him.

Love,
from your Mom, Beppe and Great Beppe.
And also from your Dad, Pake and Great Pake who keeps on encouraging you and me along life's journey.

Great Pake Rits and Great Beppe Pearl

CPSIA information can be obtained
at www.ICGtesting.com
Printed in the USA
BVHW030755280821
615510BV00006B/76

9 781602 665767